Coaching and Mentoring in Health and Social Care

The essentials of practice for professionals and organisations

Julia Foster-Turner
UK, European and International Lead
for Collaboration and Consultancy
Oxford Brookes University

Foreword by
Sir John Whitmore

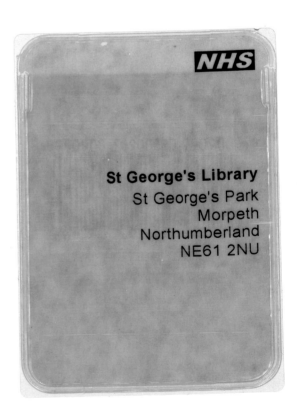

Radcliffe Publishing
Oxford ● Seattle

Radcliffe Publishing Ltd
18 Marcham Road
Abingdon
Oxon OX14 1AA
United Kingdom

www.radcliffe-oxford.com
Electronic catalogue and worldwide online ordering facility.

British Library Cataloguing in Publication Data

A catalogue record for this book is available from the British Library.

ISBN 1 85775 549 9

Typeset by Aarontype Ltd, Easton, Bristol
Printed and bound by TJ International Ltd, Padstow, Cornwall

Contents

WITHDRAWN

Foreword

Some years ago, I listened as Julia gave a brief presentation on her work to a small group at an NHS conference in Birmingham. I was impressed by her clarity and depth of understanding of the issues around coaching in the NHS and told her so afterwards. She was delighted, as she was relatively new to coaching then.

She has now produced a thoroughly thought-through clarification of what coaching and mentoring is, and a comprehensive guide to its application in the public sector. Her attention to detail is outstanding, and while it must be the definitive book in this specialist area, I would recommend it as a reference to anyone seeking to set up coaching and mentoring programmes in business or elsewhere too.

Julia helps the reader grasp the differences and similarities between coaching and mentoring, a confusing area for some, and elaborates the tools and techniques of both. Most importantly she guides us through the effective application with examples and alternatives. This is excellent work for all those who wish to bring coaching and mentoring into organisations in the public or private sectors.

Sir John Whitmore
October 2005

Sir John Whitmore was recently voted Britain's top business coach, and works with major public and private sector clients in the UK, Scandinavia, Europe, Russia and Australia. He is a best-selling author (*Coaching for Performance*, Nicholas Brealey Publishing, 2002), journalist and lecturer.

Preface

The aim of this book is to provide a solid grounding in the key principles and practice of coaching and mentoring, to help you think about your practice and what you need to consider as a mentee, coach, mentor or an initiator or sponsor of this activity within your organisation.

The concepts and techniques explored within the book draw from the knowledge and expertise of people at the leading edge of coaching and mentoring. They also cover the breadth of most coaching relationships, the organisational preparation and the context needed to support them, plus the key factors to be attended to in order to ensure quality. The following paragraphs provide some more information on how this fits within the overall shape and structure of the book.

I hope that you enjoy your reading and that it can contribute to your work in this key aspect of supporting and developing people, particularly, though not exclusively, those working within the health and social care sector.

Shape of the book

We start in Chapter 1 by exploring the world of work, as it is today, and its implications for individuals and their organisations. We will then discuss how developmental relationships have emerged and their perceive benefits and applications. This is followed by a consideration of the public sector as a context for learning and its use of coaching and mentoring. Finally, we look at what coaching and mentoring actually are, how they originated and their interrelationship.

In Chapter 2, having addressed the underlying principles and concepts of coach-mentoring, we start to consider how these apply in practice. Within the chapter, we explore how coach-mentoring relationships can be started and developed, the stages they are likely to move through and what needs to be taken into account in each of these. This chapter also provides some guidance on how you can structure individual coach-mentoring sessions, using two models developed by experts in the field.

Chapter 3 provides more information on good practice. Emphasis is placed on the understanding and use of self as the most effective coach-mentoring tool and developing the relationship. It also provides a model to help consider how to adapt your approach according to your particular mentee's/coachee's needs.

Chapter 4 contains a variety of tools, from a wide range of sources, that may be used within or outside coaching or a mentoring session. These relate to work in numerous areas, from enhancing creativity, improving self-esteem to identifying future career paths. The tools vary in complexity and potential emotional impact on those who use them, so the reader is recommended to use them with care and to test the tools on themselves before applying them to others. There is also a note of caution that any tool is a means to an end not an end in itself.

The development of coaching and mentoring schemes is currently challenging many organisations, so in Chapter 5 we examine what you need to consider in setting these up and running them well. We also celebrate some real-life examples of coaching and mentoring schemes, the learning that they share and the benefits they create.

As coaching and mentoring are such powerful tools, time is spent in Chapter 6 focusing on three key quality issues:

- the attributes, competencies and knowledge needed by people undertaking coaching and mentoring
- the supervision and support needed to develop and enhance practitioners' skills
- the ethics, standards and expectation now emerging to help guide good practice.

In the final chapter, we ask 'where now?', both for the future of coaching and mentoring and for you, whether a mentor, mentee, manager, educator, sponsor or simply someone who is interested in these forms of developmental relationships.

At the end of the book you will also find two short appendices, one containing some additional definitions of coaching and mentoring, and the other providing a list of resources such as web details of professional organisations, examples of relevant course and some additional reading.

Julia Foster-Turner
October 2005

About the author

Julia Foster-Turner is an experienced healthcare professional, manager, educator and coach-mentor with a heartfelt commitment for developing learning partnerships between both individuals and organisations.

Working within the NHS as a practitioner, with a particular interest in mental health, she developed her skills in counselling and group therapy, later moving into management and service development.

For the past six years she has been employed at Oxford Brookes University, School of Health and Social Care, involved with the development and leadership of the management education programmes, lecturing, and in providing coach-mentoring not only for UK and international students, but also for managers and practitioners within the health and social care community.

She is currently working to increase and enhance knowledge transfer and partnership between the university and other organisations in the UK and overseas.

Acknowledgements

I would like to thank Patti Stevens, my first ever and best coach. Thanks also to Sir John Whitmore and Julie Hay for their inspiring and principled approach to coaching and transformational mentoring. They have both significantly informed my practice in the art of coach-mentoring and my writing within this book. To Eric Parslow, who, among other things, has enabled me to access and use a very versatile and comprehensive network. To my friends and colleagues who have shared with me the ups and downs of writing for publication while working full time.

Most of all I would like to thank my husband, James, for his artistry and his unending patience and support over the past two years, and my daughter, Lucy, for helping me to identify what is important in life.

1

The world we live in: The context and case for coaching and mentoring

'Give me where to stand and I will move the earth.'
Archimedes (287–212 BC)

- Introduction
- The work context: issues for organisations and individuals
- Developmental relationships and their benefits
- The public sector context for learning
- Applications of coaching and mentoring
- Understanding the principles of coaching, mentoring and coach-mentoring
- Relationships between coaching and mentoring
- References

Introduction

In this chapter we explore the world of work as it is today and its implications for individuals and their organisations. We then discuss how developmental relationships have emerged and their perceived benefits and applications. This is followed by a consideration of the public sector as a context for learning, and its use of coaching and mentoring. Finally, we look at what coaching and mentoring actually are, how they originated and their interrelationship.

The work context: issues for organisations and individuals

The world of work as a whole is experiencing exponential change. The influence of the information and technology revolution, globalisation and significant societal shifts have caused employees to be thrust into a world where demands on their time and effort impinge on their non-work lives, there is less trust between employers and employees, and people are more likely than not to have several careers during their lifetime.[1]

For employers, the increasing demands of consumers, the growth of government controls and financial instability have created considerable challenges in achieving success. Related to this, recruiting and retaining the right people, with the right skills to do the job, as it is now or how it will be following the next restructure, is a major challenge to human resource management.

The Health and Social Care sectors are not immune from these pressures. Familiar challenges relate to escalating consumer expectations and demands, with inadequate resources to meet them, a limited pool from which to recruit staff and an ageing workforce. In addition, the care sector is subject to continuous monitoring of performance, outside control and political debate.

Any organisation – in the public or private sector – has to address a number of questions and challenges.

- How can it identify, deliver and maintain control of its outcomes in a world of uncertainty and frequent change?
- If an organisation needs to change itself to deliver these outcomes, how can it do so without having the right staff with the right abilities to support this change?
- As is so frequently demanded in the public sector, how can organisations maximise delivery at the point of service/care?
- How can it offer a quality service to clients/patients?
- How can it enable staff to have the time and opportunity for the development they need to meet these demands?
- How can organisations meet their own needs and at the same time the needs of the staff they value and want to keep?

The questions for employees are as follows.

- How can they maintain a reasonable quality of work–life balance and still earn enough to meet their needs?
- How do they gain personal satisfaction from what they are doing and at the same time meet the significant demands made by their employers?
- How do they stay employed or employable in conditions of decreasing job security?

It is these kinds of questions that have led to discussions about different types of relationships, working environments and ways of working, where all these needs can at least be recognised and hopefully addressed in an inclusive, mutually beneficial way, for both organisations and the individuals who work within them.

Addressing these issues through learning

Key to this emerging approach is the ability to learn. Placing ourselves within this scenario, being part of such organisations, we cannot do what we need to do, be what we need to be, unless we know how and in what way to be different and, ultimately, are able to apply this understanding to change ourselves.

There is a growing amount of literature on these questions and how to address them in the literature on learning organisations,[2] organisational learning[3] and developmental relationships,[4] in particular on coaching and mentoring.[5]

We now need to draw on some of this considerable knowledge and identify how we can apply it in order to assist learning and development within the context of a supportive organisational environment, and to the ultimate benefit of the clients and patients we serve.

Developmental relationships and their benefits

As we know from our childhood, much of our learning happens from relating to other people, such as parents, siblings and teachers. This does not stop at university or work. We soon find ourselves learning not only in more formal training workshops and courses, but also from a helpful colleague in a project team or from a mentor. These are both examples of developmental relationships.

It is interesting to note that once we have started to discuss an issue or consider a course of action in this type of relationship, we are likely to consider or interpret things in a different way. As a result, we may act or respond differently to secure a better outcome, thus demonstrating the connection between the relationship and its ability to enhance the effectiveness of the way in which we behave.

Drawing these ideas together, developmental relationships can be defined as: 'Planned or spontaneously arising relationships, through which an individual enhances their capacity to learn about themselves and their work context in order to act effectively within this.' Within such relationships, individuals are encouraged to learn from the experience of existing and novel situations, drawing on, interpreting and integrating the information these present in order to support the development of new and useful behaviours.

A reasonable question to ask at this point may be 'Do developmental relationships such as coaching and mentoring really work and what are people within the work environment using them for?'

Hall and Khan[4] suggest that careers nowadays can be considered as a number of 'learning cycles' and propose that developmental relationships are extremely effective in supporting these and in helping people to thrive in continuously changing and uncertain organisational environments. Their

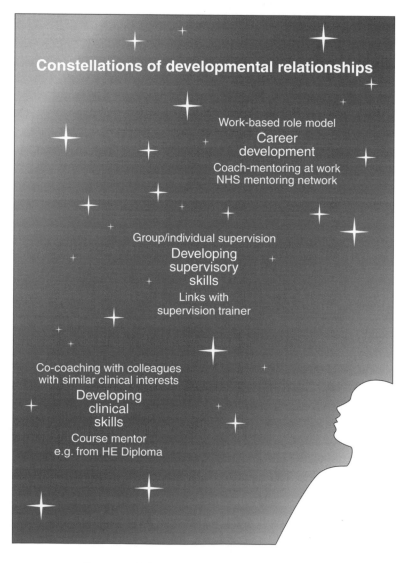

Figure 1.1   Constellations of developmental relationships.

concept is that our developmental relationships at work form a continuum that includes our role models, relationships in workshops and training programmes, in task forces and project teams, co-workers and supervisors, support groups, coaches and mentors. Along this continuum, they claim that mentoring and coaching have the highest impact on development.

Their other proposition is that people should have a network or constellation of these developmental relationships at work. Most people are likely to have a range of different working relationships that could include some or all of those mentioned above, but do not always take a co-ordinated or longer-term (strategic) view of how to make best use of them.

So perhaps we need to think in terms of how we create and use our own constellations of relationships and maybe have different constellations for different purposes at different times (*see* Figure 1.1).

Benefits of coaching and mentoring

Coaching and mentoring, as mentioned above, are very specific, focused and effective forms of developmental relationships. Later in this chapter we explore in detail exactly what these entail, but to justify *why* we should be interested, the following survey results help to point out some of the key benefits discovered so far.

A research report by the Work Foundation on Coaching[6] identified that 70% of leading employers use coaching in the workplace and that the top five benefits to the organisation were that it:

- allows fuller use of individuals' talents/potential (79%)
- demonstrates commitment to individuals and their development (69%)
- creates higher organisational performance/productivity (69%)
- increases creativity, learning and knowledge management (63%)
- motivates people (57%).

The main benefits to coaching recipients were that it:

- generates improvements in individual's performance/targets/goals (84%)
- increases openness to personal learning and development (60%)
- helps identify solutions to specific work-related issues (58%).

The following results of another recent survey by the Chartered Institute of Personnel and Development (CIPD)[7] indicates how coaching is becoming increasingly utilised and valued.

- 79% of all respondents reported that coaching was taking place in their organisations.

- 96% believed coaching is an effective way to promote learning in organisations.
- 93% believed coaching and mentoring is a key mechanism for transferring training skills into the workplace.
- 99% believed coaching delivers tangible benefits to both individuals and organisations.
- 92% of respondents believed that when coaching is applied appropriately, it can positively influence the bottom line.

In parallel to the commercial sector's interest in learning and its growing enthusiasm for coaching and mentoring, the public sector is following suit.

The public sector context for learning

In recent years, the importance of learning in health and social care organisations has been emphasised in a number of governmental strategic documents,[8–11] which have seized on the potentially positive relationship between learning and the ability for the public sector to meet its identified objectives.

It is notable that alongside the commitment to increase the numbers and skills of health and care services staff through more formal learning opportunities, such policy documents also indicate the clear agenda regarding enabling people to learn, develop and progress throughout their working lives. They also emphasise that this should happen not just through learning experiences away from base, but flexibly, within the work context itself. Additionally, this should be directed towards learning and improving performance not only in the context of direct caring relationships, but in the overall development and delivery of services in a safe, effective and integrated way.

As we will see below, even a very brief examination of government policies over the past 10 years easily demonstrates how these ideas have grown and how coaching and mentoring are increasingly used as an essential approach to deliver them.

'Working Together – Learning Together'[10] recommends 'the provision of a learning infrastructure that is accessible' and that:

- offers an opportunity for people to share knowledge
- links educational opportunities from an array of sources across NHS organisations and social services.

The paper states that such an infrastructure should encourage learning to happen through 'a variety of development methods', including '*coaching* on the job, *mentorship*, learning sets' and work experience opportunities such as 'rotations, secondments, project work as well as formal education and training'.

It also talks about services being 'learning and knowledge-based organisations', developing and sustaining 'a learning and knowledge-sharing culture ... and using extra NHS plan staff development resources better to develop *mentors*, supervisors and line managers to support their staff and teams'.[10] Developing the right environments for learning, as we shall see later, is crucial in order to enable effective learning to occur through whatever mode, and also for it to be directed specifically as needed by the protagonists, their organisation and stakeholders, especially service end-users.

In terms of formal education of healthcare professionals, despite different terms/titles being used by different professions, mentoring has long been a fundamental tool for helping people to achieve their required competencies both at pre-qualifying and post-qualifying levels. Formal and informal mentoring have also being increasingly encouraged as a way of supporting people's continuing professional development (CPD).[12]

Mentoring is also being recommended as a way of helping people to develop their new roles such as nurse and allied health profession consultants.[13] More generally, the NHS Skills Escalator[14] and the Knowledge and Skills Framework[11] have emphasised the need for structured development and performance-focused support, which in turn places considerable demand for coaching and mentoring and on developing the requisite skills to provide this.

The above-mentioned framework specifically points out that 'the commitment to the learning and development for all staff is in the context that learning which takes place in the workplace has probably not in the past been given due recognition ...'.[11] They move on to say that the commitment is to enable individuals to learn and develop in their posts throughout their lives, that it is about learning as a whole not about everyone attending a set number of hours on courses. This means people may find themselves attending fewer courses than they used to, but being helped to apply their knowledge and skills more effectively in their work.

Following this, the framework offers examples of ideas for 'on-job learning and development', 'off-job learning and development on one's own' and 'off-job learning and development with others', coaching and mentoring being cited within the first of these categories.

In light of the growing awareness of the relationship between the quality of the learning experience and professional competency development, professional bodies, such as those in nursing, have identified the need to ensure that the people who enable learning to happen, in educational facilities and practice, are highly skilled. To this end the Nursing and Midwifery Council[15] has laid down detailed, specific standards and learning outcomes for nursing and midwifery teachers' development, with greater emphasis on the role of teaching within the practice setting, alongside detailed advisory standards for mentors and mentorship, preceptors and preceptorship.

Work on enhancing such standards within the public sector is now being paralleled by the professional world of coaching and mentoring. For example, considerable work has been undertaken to develop a comprehensive set of standards for the practice of all coaches and mentors through the European Mentoring and Coaching Council. They have been exploring the idea of having a central 'core' of coaching and mentoring standards, which will be relevant to coaching and mentoring of any type, and groups of standards that relate to specific coaching and mentoring specialties.

Social work also has accessed mentoring training for some time. However, with the introduction of a more recent Social Work degree, again with greater emphasis on placement learning, there is an increased need to access learning about coaching and mentoring both for supervisors of students and those seeking support for their CPD. With regard to undergraduate learning, many of the entrants to the profession are mature and come through non-traditional access routes. Personal, though anecdotal, evidence from working with this particular type of learner has indicated that coaching and mentoring techniques have helped them to overcome the lack of confidence associated with 'returning to learning' and also to take on the challenges of balancing learning and family life.

For some time, management has also been involved in coaching and mentoring. External to the health service, executive coaching and mentoring has occupied a significant proportion of the overall coaching and mentoring market. Within the NHS, coaching and mentoring have tended to be associated with senior management and with specific management courses. Interestingly, the more recent trends in private sector coaching and mentoring have indicated a proportionately greater take-up of this kind of learning from middle managers, team leaders and supervisors, followed by professional and technical staff.[7] It will be interesting to see whether the same occurs with more junior managers and leaders within the NHS. Having had experience of running higher education management courses with integrated coach-mentoring for NHS staff of predominantly middle-management level, the potential benefit of making coaching and mentoring more widely available for this very committed, often unsupported (and considerably pressured), group of people, is evident.

There are some indications that coaching and mentoring schemes within the NHS are increasing and that healthcare providers are championing this. A real example of this is an 'Acorns Scheme', an initiative created by an innovative primary care trust. Through this scheme, any employee who has an idea about service development can take their proposal to a more senior member of staff, and if the proposal is accepted, they are coached through to achievement. This has numerous benefits. As well as supporting the member of staff's 'development through doing', it also ensures that the project is supported at senior management level – this not only reduces potential barriers to completion of service improvements, but actually makes a statement about how staff are valued.

Having pointed to the NHS focus on mentoring in senior management, a 'Mentoring Network and Mentors On-Line Database' has been developed, which is accessed through the NHS 'The Improvement Network', at www.tin.nhs.uk, and which is available to any level of staff. Through this, people can either offer themselves as a mentor or select an NHS or non-NHS mentor based on their needs and their view about what factors are important to them in a mentor. It also provides some information about the purposes of mentoring and guidelines for developing and managing mentoring and coaching relationships.

From our discussions within this introductory chapter, it seems that leaders in public sector organisations, alongside their private sector colleagues, have decided that coaching and mentoring is a realistic method for taking learning forward. It is likely that its attractiveness is due not only to its ability to utilise people's real work–life experiences and opportunities within these to support learning and development, but also to its ability to enhance performance, thus ensuring a positive impact on the quality of service delivered.

In the next section we go on to explore more specifically what coaching and mentoring can be used for and the organisational environment needed to allow coaching and mentoring schemes to grow and flourish.

Applications of coaching and mentoring

The uses of coaching and mentoring are probably limited only by our imagination, and work best whenever there is a need and desire to create positive change in ourselves, others or our environment, and where there is potential for this to be followed through by action. Figure 1.2 shows some examples of how coaching and mentoring has been used so far.

The above-mentioned CIPD[7] survey indicates that the greatest percentage of respondents reported improving individual performance as a main objective of their scheme. Many of the objectives detailed in Figure 1.2 are interrelated and, in reality, for any one scheme there is likely to be a primary objective, with a supporting group of subsidiary ones.

If you had an opportunity to develop or access a coaching or mentoring scheme, what objectives would *you* seek? Being clear about this is an important prerequisite to creating or using any scheme and can prevent serious misunderstandings and problems further down the line. We explore this further in Chapter 5.

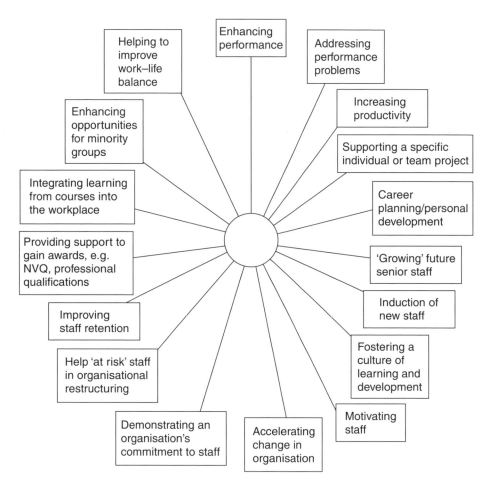

Figure 1.2   Applications of coaching and mentoring.

It is interesting to note that in terms of general principles, it is usually the context that defines for what purpose and how coaching/mentoring is provided and accessed. For example, health and social care organisations will probably be interested in schemes that are ultimately aimed at improving people's performance and productivity related to delivering their organisational objectives. Formal educational environments will have stated learning objectives and competencies for students to meet, and thus coaching and mentoring may be about helping people to achieve these.

No matter how different the context and objectives of coaching and mentoring schemes may be, they will all be founded on some common beliefs and principles about the nature of coaching and mentoring, and this is what we consider next.

Table 1.1   Your ideas about the different characteristics of coaching and mentoring

Coaching	Mentoring

Understanding the principles of coaching, mentoring and coach-mentoring

As you are reading this book, it is likely that you have an interest in coaching and mentoring and have some thoughts about what coaching and mentoring is and is not. And yet people are still struggling to define and differentiate these two terms. Thus, in a similar way to seeking clarity of coaching and mentoring objectives as mentioned above, we also need to find out what people's understanding of these terms is. This includes your own, so that you can use it as a starting point for dialogue when moving into coaching and mentoring practice.

So, without thinking too hard, brainstorm your ideas about the different nature and characteristics of coaching and mentoring and write them in the two columns in Table 1.1.

I suspect by now your will have discovered that this was not as easy a task as it first appeared. One issue is that these terms are frequently used interchangeably and often related to the specific objectives, contexts and applications under discussion at any one time. However, it is possible to draw out some common themes. One way of exploring these is to consider how coaching and mentoring concepts have emerged over time, to develop these and to see how they relate to your ideas listed above.

Mentoring

A number of books on coaching and mentoring, e.g. Parslow and Wray[5] and Clutterbuck,[16] refer to the story about Telemachus. According to legend, Odysseus asked Mentor to keep a watchful eye over his son, Telemachus, and to teach him all he knew while he was away.

Several inferences can be drawn from this.

- That someone younger, perhaps less experienced in his environment, needed someone to 'watch out' for him and 'steer him through' whatever lay ahead.
- That someone perhaps more senior and wiser could pass on their knowledge to the specific individual given to their care.

Mentoring of this kind still has much currency and value both within and outside the public sector. Large bureaucratic organisations or powerful professional groups can present political minefields for the uninitiated, and someone to advise and guide us, help us understand the political networks and culture, can help us to navigate these more effectively.

Advantages for the individual can be about survival, satisfaction and progression, for the mentor an additional sense of purpose and being valued. The organisation or professional group can benefit from achieving a more 'positive fit' between individual and organisation, an opportunity for succession planning and, hopefully, greater potential for retaining the people they want to keep.

Generally speaking, the relationship between the mentor and mentee in these circumstances may start by focusing on immediate needs of the individual, but place the emphasis on the much longer-term perspective.

Another interesting point to note is that knowledge or learning within this definition of mentoring is described as if it is something that is passed on from the mentor and received by the mentee. Today, this is certainly not the only way that people describe and understand mentoring and far greater emphasis is placed on the mentee taking much more responsibility for their own learning and the role they play within this. Also, that mentoring may come from someone 'off line', a peer or a person in a different organisation, moving more towards Hay's[17] concept of transformational mentoring.

I would suggest that there is no 'right and wrong' in how we conceive coaching and mentoring. What is important, is that as we apply these philosophies and approaches in our working environment, we ensure that the people who are involved in its practice, both at individual and organisational level, share a common understanding.

Let's move on to coaching for a moment. As I mentioned earlier, coaching is a term originally used in sport. I suspect that in your mind's eye, you could create a picture of a football coach working with the team in their practice session. He is helping them to 'go through their paces', starting with the warm-up exercises to prevent muscle injury and moving on to the finer technical skills that they need for the game. They may also work on tactics, reviewing the last game, what went well, where the problems were, considering what can be learned from the match, what can be done differently. All this is so that the team develops its players and ultimately improves its performance. Improved performance in turn will have direct, measurable outcomes, such as the number of goals scored and matches won.

Many of these ideas can be applied directly to our working environment in the health and social care sector. We need to practise and hone our skills, often in an incremental way. We need to apply these skills tactically, for a given purpose, knowing what we want to achieve, when and where. We can also learn from our successes and mistakes and use this learning to improve our performance in future. Although we can do this for ourselves, it often helps if we have someone working with us, our own coach.

The concept of coaching draws on these ideas about our learning needs and also about the relationship between coach and coachee. Remember the football coach? Go back to your mental picture of the practice session. Where is the coach? What is he or she doing? Clearly 'present' with the players, the coach could be 'egging the players on', encouraging them, getting them to do just that little bit more than they would normally do. Perhaps, depending on what is happening, being a little more prescriptive about the kind of techniques they are using, or if the session has followed a bad match, being more supportive to some of the players who need it.

Tim Gallwey, originally a sports coach and renowned for his views on coaching in the world of work, believes that we have the potential to learn how to do things, to perform them successfully, but that what often gets in the way, is our own 'interference'. Remove this and our performance will automatically improve.[18]

The kind of 'interference' he refers to is an internal critical dialogue, our judgemental 'self 1' talking to our innately able 'self 2', the result of which is to interfere with our concentration, distract our otherwise focused attention and sap our confidence. This creates a negative cycle, which builds on our failures.

He suggests that the aim of coaching is to try to reverse this process and allow our 'self 2' to focus on what it has the potential to do. To do this, Gallwey[18] proposes that we create non-judgemental awareness around what the coachee is doing; that both the coach and coachee trust in 'self 2'; and that the primary learning choices remain with the coachee.

The latter is a key concept in this approach to coaching. If the coachee can clearly define what they want to learn and how they are going to go about it, then they are more likely to be motivated to work on what they have chosen, take responsibility and be committed to achieve their goals.

In terms of roles, the coachee is responsible for learning choices and the coach for the quality of the learning environment.

Relationships between coaching and mentoring

So far we have generated some ideas about what happens in mentoring and coaching, but how do they relate to each other? We have established that both are about 'developmental relationships' in which at least one person enables the other to learn and develop. As an aside, I would imagine that any coach/mentor is also on a developmental journey alongside their 'learner'.

One way of conceiving coaching and mentoring is of them both being part of a single picture (*see* Figure 1.3). In the foreground we have coaching, geared to improving performance. The focus here may be on the shorter term, enabling the learner to identify the goals he or she wants to address, the learning that is needed for these goals to be accomplished and how this will be achieved. As we look further into the picture, towards the distance, we start to work with the learner on their longer-term aspirations. These may be fuzzy and ill defined, and perhaps our first steps would be to help them to visualise and clarify what they want and to start to think about how they will get there. This is more in line with the traditional idea of mentoring.

Figure 1.3   Coaching and mentoring as part of a single picture.

As you can imagine, there is a link between the foreground and the background, between our current goals, future aspirations, and how we can learn and develop to reach both of these.

Current goals could have implications for our future prospects, having the effect of bringing us closer to or leading us away from where we want to be in the future. This has implications when we work with people from what we have been describing here as a coaching perspective or what has been seen as a more traditional mentoring role. I would suggest that just as when we are working with clients or patients in the health and social care sector we support working with the whole person, that in coaching and mentoring, we keep both the longer-term and shorter-term perspective in view.

Regarding terminology, for the purposes of this book, due to the inter-relatedness of the two terms and because authors have used coaching and mentoring interchangeably, I will now use the term 'coach-mentoring'. This is not an original term and a definition within the Oxford School of Coaching and Mentoring journal[19] states that coach-mentoring is: 'To help and support people to manage their learning in order to maximise their potential, develop their skills, improve their performance and become the person they want to be.'

To see how other people have defined coaching and mentoring, refer to Appendix 1. A useful exercise would be for you to make a note of the definitions that you feel most comfortable with. Leave these for a period of time while you read and/or experience more of the practice of coaching and mentoring, then revisit your notes to see if your views are still the same. If they are different, consider what has influenced your views.

As we end this chapter, you have now explored:

- the relevance of coaching and mentoring in today's working environment
- the benefits that people have experienced from applying this form of developmental relationship
- the growing uptake of coaching and mentoring within the public sector
- some fundamental concepts of coaching and mentoring that form the basis for understanding and defining these terms.

The remainder of this book focuses on the key elements needed to make coach-mentoring happen within your own work environment.

References

1 Cooper CL and Burke RJ (eds) (2002) *The New World of Work. Challenges and Opportunities.* Blackwell, Oxford.

2 Senge P, Kliner A, Robert C *et al.* (1994) *The Fifth Discipline Fieldbook. Strategies and Tools for Building a Learning Organisation.* Doubleday, New York, London Toronto, Sydney, Auckland.

3 Argyris C (1992) *On Organisational Learning.* Blackwell, Oxford.

4 Hall DT and Khan WA (2002) Developmental relationships at work: a learning perspective. In: Cooper CL and Burke RJ (eds) (2002) *The New World of Work. Challenges and Opportunities.* Blackwell, Oxford.

5 Parslow E and Wray M (2000) *Coaching and Mentoring: practical methods to improve learning.* Kogan Page, London.

6 Industrial Society (1999) *Managing Best Practice: coaching report No.63.* Industrial Society (now known as the Work Foundation), London.

7 Chartered Institute of Personnel and Development (2004) *Training and Development 2004.* CIPD, London (available at www.cipd.co.uk/surveys).

8 Department of Health (1998) *A First Class Service.* Department of Health, London

9 Department of Health (2000) *The NHS Plan.* Department of Health, London.

10 Department of Health (2001) *Working Together − Learning Together. A framework for lifelong learning for the NHS.* Department of Health, London.

11 Department of Health (2004) *Knowledge and Skills Framework (NHS KSF) and the Development Review Process.* Department of Health, London.

12 College of Occupational Therapists (2004) College of Occupational Therapists: strategic vision and action plan for lifelong learning. *British Journal of Occupational Therapy.* **67**(1): 20−28.

13 Cusack L (2004) The consultant AHP. *Occupational Therapy News.* **12**(2): 19.

14 Department of Health (2001) *The NHS Skills Escalator.* Department of Health, London.

15 Nursing and Midwifery Council (2002) *Standards for the Preparation of Teachers of Nursing and Midwifery.* NMC, London. (First published by United Kingdom Central Council for Nursing, Midwifery and Health Visiting.)

16 Clutterbuck D (2001) *Everyone Needs a Mentor.* Chartered Institute of Personnel and Development, London.

17 Hay J (1995) *Transformational Mentoring. Creating Developmental Alliances for Changing Organisational Cultures.* Sherwood, Watford (UK), Minneapolis (USA),

18 Gallwey T (1974) *The Inner Game of Tennis.* Jonathan Cape, London.

19 Parslow E (2001) A definition of coach-mentoring. *Coach and Mentor.* **1**: 2.

2

A coach-mentoring framework

'The secret in getting ahead is getting started.'
Sally Berger

- Introduction
- The coach-mentoring relationship: an overview
- The coach-mentoring relationship stage by stage
- References

Introduction

Having addressed the underlying principles and concepts of coach-mentoring, we now need to know how to apply it in practice. This chapter explores how coach-mentoring relationships can be started and developed, the stages they are likely to move through and what needs to be taken into account in each of these. 'Following through the plan' also provides some guidance on how you can structure individual coach-mentoring sessions using two models developed by experts in the field.

We start by considering why we need a framework, and the aims of such a framework (Box 2.1).

Box 2.1 Coach-mentoring framework aims

- To provide an overview of the sequence of events in the life of a coach-mentoring relationship
- To provide a framework in which we can explore the coach-mentoring relationship, stage by stage, and offer a possible structure and processes for individual coach-mentoring sessions

---

The coach-mentoring relationship: an overview

The length and content of any coach-mentoring relationship can vary from one session to 18 months or more. It is defined by an agreement (overt or implied) between the mentee and coach-mentor, and will be influenced by the needs of the mentee, the time and resources of both parties, its aims and the context in which it takes place.

Although every coach-mentoring relationship will be different and tailored to individual need, this is a developmental process, which usually incorporates the stages listed in Box 2.2.

Box 2.2   Stages in the coach-mentoring relationship

1   Initiating the relationship:
   (i)   initial meeting/s to clarify purpose and process
   (ii)   preparing for the end at the beginning
   (iii)   starting to build the relationship
2   Following through the coach-mentoring relationship:
   (i)   identifying where the mentee is now and where he would like to be
   (ii)   clarifying the possibilities and options for progress, deciding on and planning a course of action
   (iii)   following through that plan
3   Reviewing progress:
   (i)   at the end of each session
   (ii)   at designated points within the period of the relationship
   (iii)   at the end of the relationship
4   Concluding the relationship

The coach-mentoring relationship stage by stage

1   Initiating the relationship

(i)   Initial meetings

The main aim of these meetings in the early stage of the relationship is to clarify what the mentee is hoping to achieve and to assess whether coach-mentoring is the best way to address this. It is an opportunity for both parties to share their understanding and expectations of coach-mentoring to see whether they will be able to relate to each other and to identify what will be important to include within a formal contract. The contract itself may or may not be completed within the first session. Unless the relationship is going to be very short, it is often useful to do this in the following session. This allows time for both parties to reflect on the initial meeting, to be clear that they are both willing to commit to the programme and to identify any unanswered questions from the initial meeting.

There is no one form of contract for a coach-mentoring relationship, although some organisations or individuals have created their own format to be used within their particular coaching or mentoring scheme. With regard to contract content, Box 2.3 offers some suggestions about the elements of the relationship that should be discussed and agreed.

Working on the contract together has the additional benefits of enabling both parties to further clarify expectations, to anticipate and prevent future problems and to provide a 'safe' opportunity to start building the relationship.

As in the rest of the coach-mentoring relationship, the aim within the process of developing the contract is to encourage the learner to work out the details and to take the 'lead' as much as possible.

Box 2.3 Elements to be discussed and referred to within a coach-mentoring contract

Names and signatures of:

- mentee
- coach-mentor
- possibly line manager/human resources manager/programme co-ordinator (insert these details when appropriate to indicate organisational support and when agreed by all parties)

Dates:

- start
- interim review
- completion of the contract

Administrative details:

- session length, frequency, venue
- contingency planning: contact details and procedure if either party has to cancel
- details of records to be kept and responsibilities relating to maintaining and storing these

Focus of contract and relationship management:

- the overall purpose of the working relationship and the key topics the mentee intends to address in the programme

- responsibilities and commitments of each party
- details of how conflict/dissatisfaction/issues within the relation-ship will be handled (by measures within the relationship and, if necessary, external to it)
- code of conduct (including dealing with matters of confidentiality)
- what will be evaluated, the form this will take and parties involved

(ii) Preparing for the end at the beginning

Whether the programme is for a day, a few months or a few years, it is important to have the end in sight right from the start of the relationship. Although this may seem a strange thing to say, it is actually a way of creating greater focus and encouragement for the mentee to achieve the goals or objectives he or she needs to within a particular time frame. It is also a way of reducing the risk of a dependency mindset as the relationship is created in the knowledge that it is of a temporary nature.

(iii) Starting to build the relationship

Although it may sound obvious, it is important to remember that any coach-mentoring relationship will stand or fall on the quality of relationship between coach-mentor and mentee. Such a relationship should be based on mutual respect and acceptance, honesty, reliability, openness and trust.

As a mentee, although we maintain responsibility for ourselves and our decisions, we come to the coach-mentoring environment expecting a safe place in which to:

- examine our mistakes as well as our successes
- take risks by exposing what we really think and feel
- experiment with ideas about what we could do.

That places the coach-mentor in a position of power. The implication of this is a requirement for the coach-mentor to act in a professional manner, not abuse their power and to act within their area of competence (*see* Chapter 6 for code of ethics, standards and expectations).

Note that if there are additional elements of power differential between coach-mentor and mentee, e.g. if this is a relationship between manager and employee or between an assessor and student, the implications of this need to be surfaced and discussed at the contracting stage, before deciding to proceed.

The first few meetings between the coach-mentor and mentee and the development of the coach mentoring contract provide an ideal opportunity in which to initiate a positive working relationship based on good communication and relationship skills (*see* Chapter 3 for more on these skills). This is also an important point to start to put into practice one of the fundamental philosophies of coach-mentoring, i.e. that the mentee is the 'real' expert in terms of knowing and addressing their own development needs and that they already hold the potential to excel. The coach-mentor's expertise need not be related to the particular issue being addressed by the mentee, but is about being able to help the mentee become aware of their situation and the choices available to them and to take the responsibility to act on these in the most effective way.[1]

This is also a stage in the relationship where you will start to become aware of the similarities and differences between the mentee and yourself as coach-mentor. To do this you, as coach-mentor, need to have furthered your own self-awareness and preferably have initiated work on your own motivations and values around coach-mentoring prior to the start of your first relationship of this kind. You also need to have some idea of your own personal learning style, because knowing this and then helping your mentee become aware of *their* learning style will help both of you to create and access the best learning opportunities for growth and development. (For guidance on self-assessment and exploration techniques, *see* Chapter 3.)

2 Following through the coach-mentoring relationship

(i) *Identifying and assessing where the mentee is now and where he would like to be*

If we are using the coach-mentoring sessions to support the development of an individual, then it will be valuable to obtain detailed information on what the mentee has done so far, as a baseline for his future development.

The content and depth of what should be explored will depend on the focus of the coach-mentoring relationship, the degree of comfort of the mentee and coach-mentor, and their available time. As a general rule, a broader understanding of the interface of different experiences and an exploration of the characteristics, impact and significance placed on these by the mentee are valuable for a number of reasons.

First, people often have little time to reflect on the range and depth of their own achievements and they forget and undervalue the personal qualities they have drawn on and the skills they have applied. Rediscovering these will not only help the mentee to know what resources they have to draw on, but should also fuel their feelings of self-esteem and efficacy, which in turn is likely to enhance their performance.

The mentee may also get in touch with things they have really enjoyed or gained great satisfaction from, perhaps creating an alternative direction for future choices. Finally, by considering actions over a period of time, patterns may emerge, both positive and negative, identifying consequences to be built on and directions to avoid.

If the coach-mentoring programme is specifically related to helping the mentee respond to a given organisational change or to learn/develop a specific skill, the gathering of information on past and current experiences and skills will be less general and instead will be oriented towards the target 'change' or 'skill'. Having said this, living and developing through change can demand a considerable range of skills, which needs to be taken into account when mentee and coach-mentor are deciding what to identify and assess.

There are a range of different tools and approaches that can be used to help the mentee to learn more about themselves, past and present and to identify future directions and the paths they can take (*see* Chapter 4 for examples of tools you can use).

(ii) *Clarify the options for progress, decide and plan a course of action*

This is where the mentee is supported to consider options and work out a plan of action. Within this process, they will draw on options that have been generated through the previous stages and consider how others can be developed. For specific skills training these options may be clearly defined. Where the mentee has broader developmental needs or complex issues, options may not be immediately obvious and further approaches may be needed to generate them, e.g. through meeting, shadowing and talking to other people, or by using more creative techniques such as those based on solution-focused therapy.

Prioritising and selecting options may be challenging in terms of identifying the selection criteria. At this point, returning to the opportunities and threats of SWOT (strengths, weaknesses, opportunities, threats) to reassess the mentee's external drivers may be important, as will using the values wheel to revisit how these options relate to meeting the mentee's values (*see* Chapter 4 for useful techniques to apply at this stage).

Where the coach-mentoring programme relates to a particular organisational issue or to specific skill development, there may be externally required targets that influence which options are selected and prioritised.

Once options have been selected, they need to be drawn together in the form of a Development Plan. This should have a section for each goal, which describes the target goal in simple but SMART (specific, measurable, achievable, realistic and time-based) terms, and the steps in terms of action/activities that will be needed to achieve it. Further refinements can be added, e.g. the resources needed to complete the activities and success criteria.

(iii)   Following through the plan

The title to this part of the process sounds very simple, but it is in fact where the mainstay of the coach-mentoring process occurs, that is where the coach-mentor supports the mentee to work on and achieve their goals over a number of sessions.

We will examine how you can structure a single coach-mentoring session shortly, but there are a number of key principles that need to be acknowledged first.

Following the mentee's agenda

- The ethos throughout coach-mentoring is about following the mentee's agenda. One of the functions of coach-mentoring is to enable the mentee to really get in touch with their true agenda, so that, based on this, they can identify and set their own clearly defined goals, which they can then explore in terms of the options for addressing them. This all has to be done at the mentee's own pace, order, etc., in a way that is meaningful and fruitful to them. If the coach-mentoring relationship falls within an organisation programme with a specific purpose, then the two agendas (of the mentee and the sponsor organisation) will have to be openly discussed and reconciled.
- The mentee's agenda may include as much work on examining why he is *not* meeting his goals as about developing and meeting them. Remember that there is no judgement and that 'failure' often creates excellent material from which to question, raise awareness and to understand and learn from.
- There may be a formalised Development Plan, which has been developed within the coach mentoring sessions or at work, that the mentee is working their way through. Hopefully, this will have been built on a careful assessment of where the mentee has come from and where they are aiming for. However, 'out of the blue', unplanned opportunities to learn may also arise from addressing incidents or other important issues from work within the coach-mentoring session. Both 'planned' and 'unplanned' or opportunistic learning are acceptable (providing this does not contradict the overall brief or balance of the coach-mentoring contract) and, in fact, can enrich the learning process.

The connection between short- and long-term plans

There is usually a connection and likely interplay between short- and long-term goals, e.g. an individual's short-term skill development may contribute to meeting their longer-term development plan. An immediate work issue and how this is addressed may have long-term implications. In the coach-mentoring process of increasing awareness and making choices, these connections need to be surfaced and taken into account.

Box 2.4   Structuring within coach-mentoring session

One of the advantages of a coach-mentoring session, is that it encourages structures in which:

- the mentee can bring to the session and/or clarify at the session his own agenda
- there is protected time and facilitation to work on this
- at the end of the session, the mentee has clarified what he needs to do to take his own agenda forward

---

The GROW model

One approach you can use to help you support the mentee in doing this within a coach-mentoring session, is to use what is called the GROW model.[1]

This sequential model stands for:

- **G**oal
- **R**eality
- **O**ptions
- **W**ill.

Using this model, the session should start with the mentee identifying a 'goal' or issue he wants to address and what he would like to have covered by the end of the session. There then needs to be time to explore the issue and identify what has happened, enabling the learner to be aware of the 'reality' surrounding it. To examine the issues in the work context, who and what is involved; to see and understand the issue from different perspectives; and to identify, question and challenge underlying assumptions.

The other half of this model is about the mentee becoming master of their own destiny – so that he can work out what 'options' may be possible and, by power of his own 'will', choose to act on these. Thus the session moves on to enable the learner to discover and broaden their range of options. Often when people think about options, they can be fairly limited, based on the way they usually do things and bounded by all the assumptions they have about how the world works. No two individuals have the same mindset, so just discussing the issues and options with the coach-mentor provides an opportunity for the mentee to question and challenge these ideas and to consider other ways of 'looking at things'.

Clarifying 'reality' and considering 'options' are all part of the process of raising awareness. 'Will' is about volition, about choosing to act, about how to act and about taking the responsibility for this choice and its resulting implications. As options are chosen and converted into a plan of action, they are defined in terms that are: Specific, Measurable, Achievable, Realistic and Time-based.

The following are some ideas for coach-mentoring questions arising from the GROW model; they have been adapted from those recommended by John Whitmore.[1]

- **Goal**: What do you want to work on/achieve by the end of this session?
- **Reality**: What has happened, is happening about this matter/issue now. What is its significance?
- **Options**: What could you do? What options have you considered and discounted and why? What options would you choose if anything were possible? What are the pros and cons of each option and which would be the best?
- **Will**: Which option/s will you act on? How does this relate to your original goal? What won't this option do? Will there be potential 'blocks' to your action and how will you deal with these? How will you know when your action has succeeded? When will you start and finish your action? Are you likely to complete any/all of these actions? What would support you to complete?

In the regular coach-mentoring sessions that follow, part of the agenda-setting and GROW process will be about gradually addressing the development plans mentioned above. The regular coach-mentoring sessions also provide an opportunity to address any *emerging* issues and agendas identified and selected by the mentee that are important to his development.

A sudden opportunity to apply for a more desirable job, a critical incident at work or a major life event may require the mentee to stop in their tracks, review their priorities and think again about where they are going and how they are going to get there. These issues can form a source of material for the GROW process, though there are other ways in which people can use them to learn.

Using a simple reflective technique

One such method would be to use a simple, written reflective technique. So, for example, with a critical incident we might: describe what happened;

think about how we felt, thought and behaved; consider what we learned; and then what we are going to do in future.

Actually writing this down helps us to: clarify our thoughts, and become more aware of our feeling and our actions; draw inferences and understanding about why we did what we did; and perhaps consider other ways in which we could have acted. Thus it allows us to learn from what we have done and identify how we would alter our responses in future.

I have used this technique many times, but it never ceases to amaze me how much more I know at the end of the process than I did at the beginning. Try it for yourself (*see* Figure 2.1).

This technique falls in line with Timothy Gallwey's recommendation from his book *The Inner Game of Work*[2] to STOP: Step back, Think, Organise your

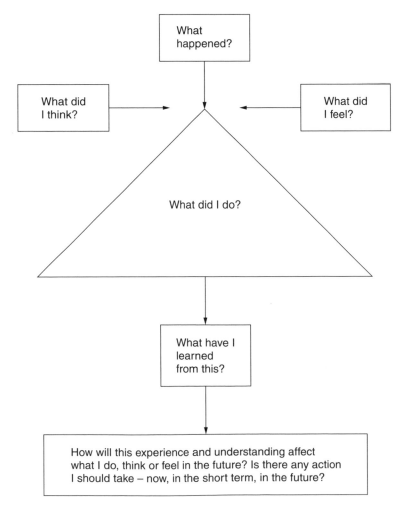

Figure 2.1 Think of an incident at work and reflect on it.

thoughts and Proceed. The advantage of STOPing is that you can do it at any level, from STOPing to allow time for reflection and strategy prior to a major career change, to STOPing to allow the possibility of a different response within an interpersonal issue.

The 3D Approach

When an issue requires an urgent response, another approach to try is the '3D Approach' devised by Eric Parslow.[3] This is fundamentally a problem-solving approach, based on the principle that to move forward we need to clarify not only what we want to achieve, but also be clear about the things that are stopping us and be able to prioritise the action needed to overcome these.

Parlsow suggests that we:

- define our problem in a single sentence
- brainstorm the hurdles around: (i) the situation, (ii) the problem and (iii) ourselves (see if you can identify three issues for each hurdle and note these down)
- then select one priority issue from each of the three aspects and note these down (these are our options)
- finally choose one or more of these priorities that are most likely to help us make progress in solving our problem.

There are many other tools and techniques that you can use within the coaching-mentoring session and I have brought together a selection of these in Chapter 3. You are not obliged to use all these tools, but their selective application can sometimes help you and the mentee overcome a block or reach into deeper personal awareness/resources. *It is important to remember that tools are a means to an end, and not an end in themselves.*

Having tested a tool on yourself you can then (if and when the moment is right) initiate its use with the mentee, by suggesting that this is something for both of you to explore. Watch carefully for your mentee's response and evidence of what seems to be helping progress in relation to this tool. Note also that each coach-mentoring relationship is different and what may have worked in one relationship will not necessarily work in another.

Keeping a record of coach-mentoring sessions

It is useful for both mentee and coach-mentor to keep a record of:

- the date
- the agenda for the session
- what has been discussed

- the action points agreed to be undertaken by the mentee and the coach-mentor
- the date, time and venue of the next meeting.

These can then be used as an aide memoir between sessions, to check progress in the following session and to use within your own supervision sessions (*see* Chapter 6). They are also useful to look back on to identify patterns of what has been successful and where there may be issues that are being processed and remain unresolved rather than being fully addressed.

3 Reviewing progress

In order to review progress, Hay[4] suggests that the mentee and coach-mentor need to consider not only progress in relation to mentee development and goals, but also the quality of the relationship and process that is enabling this to happen.

Box 2.5   When to review progress

We can review progress:

(i)   at the end of each session
(ii)   at designated points within the period of the relationship
(iii) at the end of the relationship

Reviewing progress at the end of each session

As a matter of course, towards the end of the session it is useful for both mentee and coach-mentor to discuss briefly how the session went. In particular, to provide each other with feedback about how the relationship is working and whether the session met with the expectations the learner had at the beginning of the session. The following are some prompts that you can use to help you to think about and discuss this.

Regarding the relationship:
- Consider and discuss how 'in tune' both parties felt. Did the session feel comfortable, if not, is it possible to identify where the discomfort was located?
- When there were differences of opinion or ideas between mentee and coach-mentor, were these used constructively?
- Was the behaviour of both parties professional and appropriate?

Regarding the coach-mentoring process:

- Can the mentee understand and feel comfortable with the coach-mentoring process?
- Is the process allowing the mentee to address what is relevant and important to him?
- Is the process action oriented?

(ii) Reviewing progress at designated points within the period of the relationship

Despite a good initial start to a coach-mentoring relationship, there is often a risk that such relationships can 'lose their way' and 'drift on' with no clear focus and with considerable lack of satisfaction for both coach-mentor and mentee. One way of reducing this risk or perhaps addressing these issues if they do arise, is to make best use of progress reviews.

Ideally, the timing of the reviews needs to be identified at the beginning of the relationship and noted in the contract. Within educational settings and some other environments, the rules and regulations for the relevant course or organisation will dictate the timing of these reviews. If this has not been laid down elsewhere, timing will be left to the mentee and coach-mentor to decide. Usually it is wise not to have a periodic review too early in the programme as the early stages are generally focused on exploring and cementing the relationship, and starting to understand and adapt the coach-mentoring for the mentee's specific needs.

Thus, as a guideline only, for shorter coach-mentoring programmes of say one or two months, the periodic review could be approximately half-way through. For longer-term relationships, a review every two to three months may be advisable.

Box 2.6   What to review

The review should cover three areas:

- the relationship
- the objectives and their achievement
- the process/housekeeping

Reviewing the relationship

The rationale for this part of the review is to create an opportunity to consider the relationship in the light of its ability to enable the mentee to develop, 'grow' and to take ownership in making this happen. The following are some questions to stimulate discussion in this area:

- Can both parties say what they truly think and feel?
- Can they disagree or challenge without being worried that this might be perceived negatively?
- Is the relationship encouraging the mentee's self-direction and not encouraging dependency?
- Is the learner confident about asking for what they want to meet their own needs?
- Is the mentee taking responsibility to act in order to support their own development?
- What behaviours of the coach-mentor were helpful/not helpful?
- What behaviours of the mentee were helpful/not helpful?
- Are there additional ways in which the relationship can be further enhanced/more effective?

Reviewing objectives and their achievement

The aim of this section is to revisit and check agreement about what the perceived objectives are, assess progress against these and realign them if necessary. In some cases this is a fairly simple process. However, it can be made more complicated by the fact that coach-mentoring can be set up with varying degrees of clarity regarding the objectives of the relationship.

Where specific objectives have be outlined from the start (within the contract), e.g. relating to defining potential career paths, adopting to a changed work environment or developing specific skills, these may be relatively easy to measure.

Where the relationship has less clearly defined objectives, e.g. around the need to support self-development, say over a given period of time, and where perhaps learning has been through exploring and building on how current issues are addressed, then 'achievement' of goals may be more diffuse. However, the review will be an important time to reflect back, discuss and mark where learning has occurred and where this has enabled the individual to create positive change within them. It may also create an opportunity to make future goals more specific.

This is also a time to consider whether there are patterns of issues that keep coming up which are not getting addressed in the sessions. Do these need some agreement that they will be responded to or do both parties come to an agreement that there *is* an issue, but that this *will not* be addressed within the coach-mentoring sessions?

More broadly, the review is also a time to question whether the original objectives are still completely relevant or if they need adjusting or changing altogether.

Where objectives and the overall programme have been closely linked with the organisation, it *may* be appropriate to involve relevant people from the organisation for part or all of the review process. The potential for, and appropriateness/acceptability of this, needs to be discussed at the development of the overall programme within the organisation and with *all* parties at the contractual stage of the relationship.

Reviewing process and housekeeping

The final, but very important, element of the coach-mentoring review is related to the practical process of meeting and working together. The following are points to consider.

- Within the sessions – does the process allow for the mentee to address what they need to? Is the balance of the time spent on follow-up from the previous sessions, exploration of current issues and action planning working well? Does the format of the sessions allow flexibility when this needed? Is the process used clear to the mentee?
- Which communication skills used by the coach-mentor are effective and which communication skills less effective?
- Which techniques and tools that the coach-mentor uses are helpful? Which techniques and tools that the coach-mentor uses are less helpful/not helpful?
- What further skills would it be helpful for the coach-mentor to apply.
- Is the spacing of sessions such that there is enough time between them for the mentee to work on what they need to do, but close enough together so that momentum can be maintained and actions followed through?
- Do both parties come to sessions adequately prepared?
- If parties have to adjust meeting times or cancel, is reasonable notice given when possible, are contact methods working, e.g. through phone or email? Have there been many cancellations? If so, why?
- Is the environment selected for the sessions appropriate? Does it provide a space that is quiet, uninterrupted, adequately ventilated, etc?
- How can these processes/housekeeping elements be improved?

(iii)   *Reviewing progress at the end of the relationship*

As mentioned earlier, the end of the relationship should be something that has been prepared for from the start. Nevertheless, it often comes as a shock and it can be somewhat distressing that the coach-mentoring relationship is coming to an end. So, in addition to this final review being around the objectives and content of the programme and the relationship that has supported it, it has the special function of 'closure' and managing all the emotions that this may entail.

Many of the questions that were mentioned in 'Reviewing progress at designated points within the period of the relationship' will be relevant. The coach-mentor will need feedback on their approach, this time not for taking the relationship forward, but perhaps more for learning to improve their skills and techniques for future work. The mentee will be interested in discussing their progress around their objective, but will have additional concerns about 'what now?'

The following topics may be used to structure your session.

Mutual feedback on:
- what has been particularly helpful about the working relationship
- the challenges within the relationship
- any additional feedback thought to be helpful at this point.

Review of objectives and achievement:
- progress against initial and periodic reviewed objectives
- any memorable events and points of significant personal learning
- celebrations of success.

Plans for the future:
- from the perspective of the mentee. How is the mentee's personal development going to continue? What would be three key priority actions in doing this?
- from the perspective of the coach-mentor. In a similar vein, how is the coach-mentor going to take what they have learned from this relationship forward?
- is there any learning from the experience that can be shared, e.g. links with the wider coach-mentoring or organisational community?

Final goodbyes and thanks
- This is fairly self explanatory, but often quite difficult to do. It is important to acknowledge that in some relationships there may well be a significant feeling of loss and that this is to be expected.
- There may also be thoughts of what could have been in the minds of both parties. Some of this may be addressed in the 'Plans for the future', but part of these final conversations may be about coming to terms with and accepting 'what has been' and 'what is now'.

4 Concluding the relationship

Much of this has been covered in the previous section. In addition, the coach-mentor should undertake a final reflection on the relationship to ensure that as much learning as possible is achieved and acted upon. This may also be the point, if relevant, at which to contact and confirm with the organisational programme co-ordinator that the relationship has come to a close, to feedback on any non-confidential organisational process issues and to ensure the notes continue to be stored in a confidential manner.

There are some occasions when the mentee asks to extend the relationship, in which case careful consideration needs to be made about the reasoning behind this and whether it is thought to be appropriate (assess possible issues/risks relating to the relationship continuing, such as dependency).

If this is the case, then a new contract should be developed to clarify that this is a new stage in the relationship and that its function is clearly defined.

References

1 Whitmore J (2002) *Coaching for Performance* (3e). Nicholas Brealey, London.

2 Gallwey T (2000) *The Inner Game of Work*. Orion, London.

3 Parslow E and Wray M (2000) *Coaching and Mentoring: practical methods to improve learning*. Kogan Page, London.

4 Hay J (1995) *Transformational Mentoring. Creating Developmental Alliances for Changing Organisational Cultures*. Sherwood, Watford (UK), Minneapolis (USA).

3

Skills and good practice in coach-mentoring

'Keep your feet on the ground and keep reaching for the stars.'
Casey Karem

- Introduction
- Coach-mentoring self-awareness
- Communication and relationship skills
- An adaptive approach to enabling through coach-mentoring
- References

Introduction

Having introduced the broader concepts of coach-mentoring and discussed a framework in which to use them, we now need to consider the skills and practices that help coach-mentoring work well.

The most important coach-mentoring tool that you have is yourself, thus the emphasis of this chapter and our starting point is self-awareness and relating effectively within the coach-mentoring relationship. We will then move on to addressing coach-mentoring from the mentee's perspective through 'An adaptive approach to enablement'. Drawing on current knowledge this offers a flexible model through which to consider your approach to coach-mentoring.

Coach-mentoring self-awareness

Separating your needs from those of your mentee's

Although much good coach-mentoring practice is about the content and quality of the relationship and the dialogue between coach-mentor and mentee, the first 'skill' we need is that which enables us to examine *ourselves*. The reason why this is important, is that unless we are aware of ourselves and our motivations, the latter can 'leak' into the coach-mentoring relationship and potentially subjugate the needs of the mentee to those of our own, at considerable expense to the coach-mentoring relationship and its effectiveness.

Checking the match between your beliefs and values and the coach-mentoring mindset

It is also important to consider ourselves in relation to the coach-mentoring 'mindset', the foundation of beliefs on which effective and appropriate coach-mentoring is based and which were introduced and briefly discussed in the first chapter.

Understanding our learning styles

If we hope to enable other people to learn, we need to make sure that we understand the learning process and take into account that different people may approach this learning process in different ways. Thus coach-mentor and mentee may have different learning styles.

It is important to be aware of this so that we apply learning opportunities in a consciously selected way, because they take into account the learning style and needs of our mentee, rather than selecting the style that we have found beneficial for ourselves.

The following is an opportunity to reflect on your self-awareness in the area of your own personal needs and motivations, values and beliefs and learning styles in a little more detail.

A coach-mentor's self-assessment

1 Our needs and motivations as coach-mentors

Consider the questions in Box 3.1 and note down your answers. As you answer, try to identify your responses in terms of your thoughts (T), your feelings (F) and any relevant actions (A).

Box 3.1

1 Why do I want to become involved in coach mentoring?

(T)

(F)

2 What will I hope to gain from the relationship?

(T)

(F)

3 What do I think may be the negative aspects of such a relationship and how would I handle these?

(T)

(F)

(A)

4 Is there any conflict of interest between my engagement in coach-mentoring and my other relationships/responsibilities inside and outside of the organisation? If so, what action should I take?

(T)

(F)

(A)

5 What will be the source of my support and supervision? What action will I need to take to arrange/access this?

(T)

(F)

(A)

6 Is there anything else concerning me about this? If so, how should I proceed?

(T)

(F)

(A)

As you work through this list, you will be enhancing your own self-awareness and developing a simple reflective technique that you will be able to use with your learner. Start by working through these questions alone and then take you answer to a trusted 'critical friend', one who you believe will be willing to challenge you.

One reason for taking this approach is that discussing these matters may reveal any 'blind spots' you may have. The other reason is for you to be reminded of what it is like to reveal your thoughts and feelings to someone else. Note the importance of 'trust'. I would imagine the person you selected to discuss your 'list' with, was someone with whom you have established a trusting relationship over a period of time. Consider how this is relevant to your future coach-mentoring relationship.

2 Our values and beliefs as coach-mentors

Moving on from these initial questions, we need to consider the following statements. They have been adapted from Julie Hay's book on transformational mentoring,[1] and they incorporate some fundamental beliefs on which we can build our coach-mentoring relationships.

- We are all valuable and merit concern.
- It is normal to want a genuine relationship with other people.
- People are unique.
- Everyone has the ability to change.
- Given the information, we are the best arbitrators of our own decisions.
- People have an innate desire to develop and realise their potential.
- Different people have different understandings of the world and how it works.
- People usually do things for a reason no matter how obscure this may initially appear.

Consider how these views relate to your own mindset and experiences in life.

3 Learning styles

Think about the people you have worked or studied with. Have you noticed that some individuals in a novel situation will immediately try working within it and test things out, others will sit at a distance and reflect on ways in which the situation could be approached, others may find a book on the subject, and so on? This illustrates the diverse ways in which people learn.

In coach-mentoring, where the key focus is on learning and development, knowing the way your mentee learns is essential.

Of equal importance is the need for you to explore and understand your own learning style. Why is this? There are two main reasons:

First, as a coach-mentor you will be expected to continually develop yourself, thus knowing how you learn best will help you to do this more effectively. It also provides you with an opportunity to identify where you can expand your learning skills.

Second, in terms of the coach-mentoring relationship, if you are unaware of your own learning style you may be encouraging your mentee to utilise a certain style not because it is the most suitable for the mentee, but because you may have unconsciously selected the style that most suits you. (An inference from this statement is that raising your own self-awareness allows you to make better choices about what you do. When we are working in the role of coach-mentor, raising self-awareness is an important tool we can use with the mentee.)

The learning process

Kolb,[2] an American psychologist, identified learning as a cyclical process (*see* Figure 3.1).

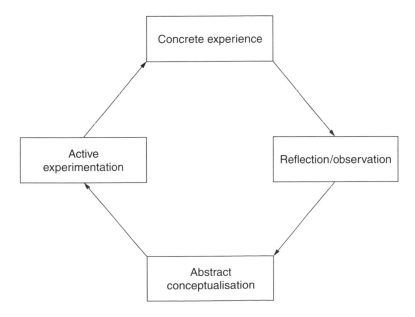

Figure 3.1   The Kolb learning cycle.

He suggested that in real life:

- we have intentional or accidental 'concrete' experiences
- we reflect on these to understand their meaning and significance, from this
- we create concepts, structures of understanding, theories and rules that will influence our future expectations, and then that
- we try out these explanations and rules in the process of active experimentation.

These create our experiences which then move back into the learning cycle.

Honey and Mumford[3] developed these ideas further and identified that each of us are more skilled in some stages of the cycle than others and that this will influence our learning preferences. Thus most people will have a predominant style and can be classified as activists, reflectors, theorists or pragmatists.

- **Activists** learn by doing, with no clear attempt to understand or analyse what is happening. They enjoy getting into new experiences and taking on problems and challenges. They learn best in the here and now, when there is risk and pressure and they can work with other people.
- **Reflectors** like to watch and listen, they draw in and assimilate information. They learn best when they are given time to think, have all the information they need and they have time to make decisions.
- **Theorists** learn by abstracting rules, theories and generalisations and use these to direct their future actions. They like objectivity and logic, learning best when they can use models to clarify their understanding and can explore connections and relationships between ideas and facts.
- **Pragmatists** focus on applying ideas to practice in the real world. They learn best when they can test things out and the link between theory and the real world is clear.

Consider which learning style most closely relates to your approach to learning. Brainstorm a list of the learning activities that you have undertaken in the past month. How do these relate to the style that you have identified?

Box 3.2   Developing your learning style

Is there a learning style that you would like to practise more? If so, discuss this with a colleague or friend. Plan and note in your diary an opportunity to do this within the next month. Discuss how the experience went and how you felt about it with you colleague or friend. What have you learned from this experience that may influence how you help others to learn?

You have now spent some time on your personal development as a coach-mentor. Just as with other aspects of your work, to be an effective and safe practitioner in coach-mentoring, you will need to assess and meet your development needs on a continuous basis.

A helpful practice is to find a coach-mentor for yourself. This has the benefit of enhancing your own skills and development at the same time as learning about coach-mentoring through experience.

Supervision, experienced individually or as part of a group, is also good practice and should be a 'given' of any reputable coach-mentoring scheme (*see* Chapter 5). You may also wish to consider formal training. For a list of useful contacts, *see* Appendix 2.

Communication and relationship skills

Communication

Having examined ourselves and started to gain a greater self-awareness, we will now move on to considering how we are going to communicate with and relate to our mentee. So, on 'communication' within this section we will explore:

- the process of communication
- risks to communication
- non-verbal communication
- what helps to make communication work well
- being there, listening and responding.

These communication skills will benefit the mentee most when they are used within a relationship built on strong foundations of the warmth, acceptance and empathy we have for our mentees, and the openness, honesty and reliability in the way we behave towards them. Thus these will be discussed following our work on 'communication'.

The process of communication

As employees working within health and social services environments, we spend a considerable number of hours communicating with clients and patients, other colleagues and an array of different agencies. Many of us have undergone professional training and further development that has incorporated communication skills, and yet knowing the ideals and managing to practise them are a continual challenge. The following sections give you an opportunity to revisit some of the key principles and consider their application within a coach-mentoring context.

Two-way communication

Let's start with a straightforward situation where two people, Lucy and Laura, are sitting in a room for the purpose of a discussion (Figure 3.2). What are the steps that are happening within the communication process?

Figure 3.2 Two-way communication.

In essence, we could say:

- Step 1: Lucy generates thoughts and feelings (based on her relationships and other experiences that have developed her view of the world)
- Step 2: Lucy selects and clarifies what she wants to communicate to Laura
- Step 3: Lucy forms this into words that she feels comfortable using (generated from the particular national, organisational and professional culture in which she has developed)
- Step 4: Lucy communicates these, by speaking to Laura
- Step 5: Laura hears what is said
- Step 6: Laura interprets the words based on her understanding of the meanings attached to the words used

- Step 7: Laura also takes her perception of the overall message and relates this to her view of how the world works
- Step 8: this arouses thoughts and feelings in Laura.

Laura then responds through the same process, and so on.

As a brief exercise, brainstorm what you think may be the risk factors linked with these steps.

Box 3.3 Communication risk factors

Step number(s)   *Communication risk*

Potential risks

Box 3.4 shows some risks that I have identified.

Box 3.4   Examples of communication risk factors

Step number(s)	*Communication risk*
1 and 7	Lucy and Laura's constructs (view of the world) may be different to the extent that they are not compatible.
2	Lucy may not have formulated her ideas clearly, which may make them open to misinterpretation.
3 and 6	Lucy and Laura may have different interpretations or meanings attached to the same words. This may be different because of cultural reasons or, possibly, there may be personal meanings that Lucy or Laura give to a particular word that the other party does not share and is unaware of. Poor understanding of language may also be linked to different levels of linguistic competence, e.g. if the language used is not the first language for both Lucy and Laura.
4 and 5	If there are physical problems, regarding speaking or hearing, in one or both parties.

Let's move on from generalities and link this with your own experience. Take a real conversation that you had with someone else that did not go as well as you had expected. Using the same framework, try to identify where, in the steps that we have explored, the communication problems arose, what they were and, in the final column, what approach, if any, could have been taken to prevent or lessen the problem?

Box 3.5   Identifying communication problems and planning how to prevent them

Step number(s)   Communication problem   Preventive action

Non-verbal communication

The other factor that could have influenced the conversation that you used in the previous exercise is non-verbal communication. This and its relationship with verbal communication will significantly influence the quality of your coach-mentoring relationships in the future.

Mehrabian[4] states that when we communicate with each other, the message about our feelings and our attitudes comes 7% from our words, 38% from our voice and 55% from our bodies.

Non-verbal communication can support and emphasise what we are communicating verbally, but if there is a perceived difference between our verbal and non-verbal communications, people are more likely to believe the non-verbal message.

So, in our coach-mentoring relationship we will need to take note of non-verbal communication and any conflicts between verbal and non-verbal communication we see in our learner. We will also need to act with care, as there is a possibility of misreading what we hear or see. One way to avoid this is to look for more than one action that is appearing to communicate the same message and, most importantly, to check our perceptions, sensitively, with our mentee.

What helps to make communication work well

Having considered the steps involved in the communication process and where potential risk factors may emerge, we now need to consider communication in terms of its role in bringing two people together.

Box 3.6   What makes communication work well?

Think about a time when you spoke to someone who you felt really understood you.

- Why do you think this was?
- What was it that they did or said?
- What was your response to this?

Three fundamental communication elements are those of:

- being there
- listening
- responding.

Being there

Being there is 'attending', it's about keeping your attention within the conversation you are having, rather than allowing your mind to drift off to the next meeting or a future visit to the supermarket, for example. It maintains your concentration so that you can listen and understand what is being said and be able to respond. This in turn also communicates to the mentee that you value what they have to say.

Egan[5] suggests that we utilise the following 'microskills', remembered through the acronym SOLER.

- **S, Sit squarely**, so that you are upright and not slouching. This will indicate that your are concerned about what your listener has to say.
- **O, Open posture**, sit with your arms and legs uncrossed, indicating that you are being 'open' rather than defensive.
- **L, Lean slightly forward** periodically according to the flow of conversation. This again indicates your engagement in the communication process.
- **E, Eye contact**, keep this consistent, but not a constant stare. A fixed gaze can be perceived as threatening.

- **R, Relax**, this will indicate that your are confident about your knowledge and skills. Try to be comfortable and at ease with your learner. A cautionary note, however, is that looking over-relaxed may be interpreted as boredom.

Listening and understanding

Listening is not a natural phenomenon like hearing. We often *have to* hear sounds and other peoples' conversations whether we like it or not. In contrast, listening is an activity we *choose* to do and it takes considerable energy and practice to maintain our focus, to remember, to make sense of and to understand what is being said.

In the process of understanding we may communicate what we think is being said to check that our understanding is accurate and to enable the mentee to expand on this.

As we listen, we also need to become conscious of our own personal responses to what is being said, both in terms of our emotions and thoughts, and to be able to perceive these separately from those of the mentee. This does not prevent us from using our own intuition and instincts to facilitate the coach-mentoring process, but it does need to be done with caution.

Thus in these circumstances we must continuously check our understanding of the meaning of what is being communicated and the inferences that can be drawn for this with the mentee.

This is good practice in any working relationship and underlines the philosophy that within the coach-mentoring relationship it is the *learner* who holds the knowledge and expertise needed to understand and address their own needs, the coach-mentor's principle function being to create an appropriate environment that facilitates such learning.

Responding

Responding is about communicating to our learner that we have received their message. Egan[5] suggests that the proof of good listening is good responding.

We need to listen, and in our response indicate that we have understood the whole message that our learner is giving us, that we recognise how he or she is feeling and how this is related to their interaction with the world around them.

Our response can be in the form of questions, which indicate that we want to understand the situation or problem clearly. The questioning can be done in such a way that we use the questions to help the mentee to clarify the issue for themselves. For example, 'You say that you have no time to work on this particular project, tell me more about the time you would need ...'.

A risk with questioning is that you can lead someone away from the crux of what they wanted to work on. There is also a possibility of using it as an obscure way to give advice or criticism.

You also need to ensure an appropriate balance in the use of open and closed questions. So, for example, when you are seeking specific information or a 'yes' or 'no' answer, closed questions are appropriate. But if you are encouraging your mentee to explore the implications or options around a particular decision, open questions may be a preferred option.

Before we leave this section, Box 3.7 gives some useful kinds of responses that you can use to different effects.

Box 3.7   Useful types of response

Summarise what has been said
This is helpful to show that you have been listening, to check understanding and also to draw the threads of the discussion together and allow the conversation to move on.

Examples
'So, let's see where we have got to ...?'
'If I can summarise that ...'

Echo the last phrase of what the mentee said
If you do this then leave a pause, it can encourage the mentee to elaborate further.

Example
'The situation has become intolerable' PAUSE ...
(Paralanguage such as 'um', 'uh-uh' can also be used to encourage your mentee to say more.)

Rewording
This indicates that you understand what is being said and helps to clarify and maintain focus on the issue.

Example
Original statement: 'Laura is driving me mad, she expects me to do half a dozen jobs, and I'm already doing two people's jobs.'
Rewording: 'You are very angry about what Laura is expecting you to do, especially with your current high workload.'

Create greater focus

You may also create greater focus, by bringing the mentee back to something they have said and asking them to say more about it.

Example

'You mentioned the issue to do with workload, this is obviously concerning you a great deal at present, can you tell me a little more about what effect this is having on you ...?'

Foundations of the coach-mentoring relationship

Listening, understanding and responding are all parts of developing good communication and dialogue between you and your mentee. This will happen most effectively in a coach-mentoring relationship developed on strong foundations. These are the *warmth, acceptance* and *empathy* we have for our mentees, and the *openness, honesty* and *reliability* in the way that we behave towards them.

The following paragraphs are used simply as an opportunity to introduce these concepts and to invite you to reflect on how you engage these within your own relationships.

Warmth and acceptance

Warmth is about being welcoming, approachable and emanating a positive feeling. Acceptance means accepting people for who they are, even when what they do or the values they display do not fit into your view of what is acceptable or 'normal'. We need to accept people not for what they can do or their position in life, but for who they are.

It is also likely that in order to accept others, we need to accept ourselves!

Empathy

McBride and Maitland[6] describe empathy as 'the basic building block of positive relationships. It is the ability to recognise and respond to other people's fears, concerns and feelings.'

It is often described as the ability to stand in someone else's shoes.

Why do we need empathy in coach-mentoring?

The agenda of coach-mentoring is essentially led by the mentee, so in order to help them work through this, we need to have the ability to 'be there' with them. Empathy helps us to do this and also to communicate more effectively, as we will be communicating from the perspective of the mentee's experience rather than our own.

Our ability to be in touch with the emotions that our mentee is experiencing also helps us to be more aware of when to change our style of intervention, e.g. from being challenging to being more supportive.

Often empathy requires us to be able to tune into the clues apparent in another individual, and can range from noticing or looking for body language, to enquiring about and acknowledging other people's feelings.

It is possible for us to empathise by simply taking the perspective view of another person, i.e. *cognitive* empathy. However, it is possible to experience *emotional* empathy, where we actually feel what the other person is feeling. For example, if your mentee was in a state of outrage because of an incident with their manager, you could also experience these feelings. A risk here, particularly if you are unaware of what is occurring, would be for it to lead you to encourage or support an inappropriate response. However, you may acknowledge this anger, both within the mentee and in yourself, and create an objective platform from which the mentee could start to identify their learning and future actions.

Responding to someone in an empathetic way can provide varying degrees of challenge! Consider how you would respond to the individual in the following scenario.

Someone who you are coach-mentoring has just arrived late for the third time in a row. His first comments are to complain that he is feeling really frustrated about your scheduling of the sessions.

A response without empathy might be based on asking yourself why this person did not say that the schedule was unacceptable when first presented with it. You may perhaps come to the conclusion that this person is disorganised and is complaining about the schedule as an excuse for arriving late. A response with these thoughts in mind may incorporate some element of criticism.

But if you start by suspending judgement and placing yourself in your mentee's shoes (experiencing the feelings associated with arriving late and feeling so frustrated with the schedule), your response is likely to reflect this and to set a more construct tone to deal with this and other issues.

Empathy is a skill that can be developed through practice. Try at least once a day, to concentrate on the emotional as well as on the material content of a conversation and note the impact this has on your responses.

Openness

This involves being honest and clear with yourself and your mentee. We have already touched on self-examination, being clear about our own motives and values. Without this awareness we cannot question what we think, feel and do in order to make choices about what we will do and how we will act in future.

We also need to be able to use this awareness of ourselves, the context in which we are coach-mentoring, e.g. the organisational context, and what we discover about the mentee himself in an open and honest way that does not put the mentee at any disadvantage. This will impact on what we say and do both within the coach-mentoring relationship and outside of it.

In practical terms, these issues need to be discussed as part of the process of developing a formal coach-mentoring contract, revisited within coach-mentoring sessions, and monitored in supervision and in the review of the coach-mentoring contract.

Consider:

- the commitment to confidentiality by both coach-mentor and mentee
- other roles or relationships either the coach-mentor or mentee has that may influence what can be addressed or disclosed by either party
- what will be covered, in terms of feedback by both parties, on the process and content of the coach-mentoring sessions
- how dissatisfaction in the relationship will be dealt with.

Self-disclosure

Another aspect of 'openness' relates to the practice of disclosure. Although coach-mentoring is directed towards developing the mentee, and self-disclosure as a tool to self-knowledge is an assumption on which coach-mentoring is based, we too need to be able to disclose something of ourselves.

Thus, within the coach-mentoring process, the coach-mentor reveals something about themselves and the mentee may also share something about themselves. This is not an alternating 'tit-for-tat' process, but the fact that they have reciprocated will move the relationship to a deeper level and makes further self-disclosure more likely.

Self-disclosure can be done at many levels, from sharing our name to information about relationships and experiences. The degree to which self-dislcosure is used is very personal and is influenced by our upbringing and culture as well as our gender (women are said to be more willing to disclose than men!).

Within the coach-mentoring relationship, the depth of disclosure is related to how safe and confident one individual feels with the other; it should be appropriate to the discussion at hand and not place the mentee at an emotional or practical disadvantage.

Being honest and reliable

These are probably taken as 'given'. However, in a stressful life with a number of competing priorities, the challenge to maintain complete honesty and reliability may be more difficult than it first appears. Commonly, issues are around keeping commitments, e.g. regarding appointments, and undertaking the actions agreed at the end of the coach-mentoring session.

Acting in an honest and reliable way within a relationship helps to build and maintain trust. We can use the analogy of the trust between two people being like a shared bank account. We can make a deposit in the 'trust' bank balance by meeting our commitments, but if we let someone down, we make a withdrawal. Enough 'contribution' has to be made to maintain this joint account.

An adaptive approach to enabling through coach-mentoring

Within a relationship at work or at home, the way that we behave towards each other may change from day to day or even hour to hour. Often our behaviour is dependent on the goals of the relationship at any one point in time, and behaviours that each member of the relationship has found to be successful in helping them meet similar goals before.

It is noticeable that in relationships that work well, there is 'responsiveness' – where either or both parties seek to identify the other member's current state in terms of their thinking, how they are feeling and also their needs and goals.

The coach-mentoring relationship utilises the attributes of such a 'responsiveness', but, in addition, clarifies and structures the roles within it, so that the primary focus for the mentee is to identify and achieve their goals and the focus for the coach-mentor is to enable them to do this. To be able to

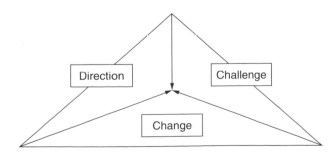

Figure 3.3   An adaptive approach to enabling.

'enable', just as in other positive relationships, the coach-mentor needs to take into account the mentee's current 'status' – how the mentee is thinking and feeling, and also what they are trying to achieve and their level of skills and experience in relation to this.

To be able to 'enable' the coach-mentor thus needs to be responsive and *adapt* their *approach* in accordance with the needs, abilities and goals of the mentee.

In varying our approach we need to think about three key aspects (Figure 3.3):

- how *directive* we are
- how much we *challenge* our mentee
- how we help our mentee grow and develop through *change.*

Let us explore these three areas in more detail.

How directive are we?

The extent of direction we give people within the coach-mentoring relationship will vary according to our personal approach as coach-mentors and the nature, needs and environment of the individual. As coach-mentor we need to be aware of the extent to which we are being directive and non-directive and whether this is in line with the needs of the mentee (Figure 3.4).

The level of direction provided will influence the amount of choice offered to the mentee within the learning experience and consequently may affect the amount of responsibility the learner is able or willing to hold for their own learning process. As in coach-mentoring we are trying to encourage the mentee to take responsibility for their own learning. We should therefore be supporting greater use of learning processes that occur at the less directive end of the continuum.

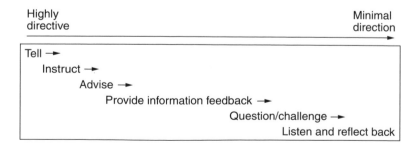

Figure 3.4   Extent of direction given within the coach-mentoring relationship. Adapted from Downey.[7]

There will, clearly, be times when for the purpose of learning a skill, a more directive approach is necessary. As that person moves from novice to expert in that area, the level of direction can be decreased.

Think about your current work in developing other people either at home or at work over the last two weeks. How directive and non-directive were you?

Box 3.8   Could you assess the percentage of time you spent in the different levels of 'direction'?

Degree of direction   *Percentage time*

Tell
Instruct
Advise
Provide information/feedback
Question/challenge
Listen and reflect back

Box 3.9   Alternative ways of relating

Thinking back, was there a specific instance where you could have offered less direction? If so, what would you have done differently?

The degree of challenge offered

Challenge within the context of coach-mentoring is about how much challenge we provide for the mentee. We can consider this from two perspectives.

1   Challenging the mentee's mindset, questioning existing ideas and assumptions.
2   Creating challenge that encourages the individual to go a little bit further into unknown learning territory and to try for goals which at present may seem out of reach.

Perspectives 1 and 2 are interrelated, as perspective 1 offers the benefit of altering or extending the realm of possibilities in which the mentee sees themselves and in which they currently function. The impact of the mentee believing that they can access these possibilities improves their self-efficacy, and will actually increase what they are likely to achieve, thus supporting them to address the challenge within perspective 2.

1   Challenging assumptions

In coach-mentoring these assumptions may, for example, be related to someone's skills, potential or the environment in which they currently or could work in future. One of the first steps is to 'find' these assumptions and bring them to the surface. This is less difficult than it seems and opportunities are likely to arise throughout the coach-mentoring sessions.

Imagine, for example, someone says that there are no opportunities for their progression. On discussing this further within a coach-mentoring session you discover their assumptions are that:

- only certain of their skills and experience will have 'progression' currency
- the only kind of progression is the next step up in the chain of command
- their skills are not transferable elsewhere
- they are not highly valued.

The next step is to ask what evidence there is for each of these assumptions, and if there is none, to encourage the mentee to consider and explore what alternatives could possibly exist. Regarding the last assumption, for example, we may find that the mentee has no evidence that they are not valued. In addition, we discover the mentee had thought that the other people in their team had moved on because they were valued and they, the mentee, was not, and thus had been left behind.

They were challenged to question the automatic link between their lack of progress and not being valued – that the lack of progress may have been related to the fact that they perhaps needed to put themself forward, rather than wait to be asked and that perhaps this had already started to come into their subconscious as they were starting to think about moving on.

2   Creating the challenge

Most people, as they experience the coach-mentoring process, share some of their very special hopes and dreams. These are often expressed as being slightly out of reach or even unobtainable. Frequently, but not always, the block to someone attaining these dreams is at least partly in their own mind.

Our job as coach-mentors is to help the mentee identify their aspirations and to draw out these apparent 'impossibilities' within them.

These are the challenges that will stretch and develop the mentee. They are too great to reach instantly and easily, but will create the challenge and motivate our mentee as they are founded on what the mentee really values and desires.

To challenge or not to challenge

Challenge incorporates the aspect of risk. As your coach-mentoring relationship develops you will start to have an understanding of the level of risk with which the individual feels comfortable.

Some mentees may find it hard to even consider the possibility that some of their long-held assumptions could be questioned. Others may have no issue with this, but have dismissed some of their less conventional ideas on possibilities for the future and created a very finite view of the world that they may not wish to disturb.

There are no clever answers on to how to address this. When we struggle to identify a way forward, it is easy to start judging, and to say that an assumption is 'wrong' and that the mentee 'should' respond in a certain way or take a particular course of action. Remember, these are your 'rights' and 'wrongs', which are not important. Step out of your shoes and into your mentee's to be directed.

A wise approach is to ensure a sound, trusting relationship and to take your mentee's lead in selecting their agenda. When opportunities to challenge arise, such challenge can be *offered*, with respect. If the mentee accepts this offer, proceed in small steps, so that you can constantly check that your mentee is comfortable with the ground they are covering and the approach you are using.

To support rather than challenge

Note also, that sometimes people within a coach-mentoring relationship may be experiencing difficulties at home or at work. They may be vulnerable and instead of needing challenge, will need you to show caring and concern. Your approach within this scenario may be to focus on maintaining or enhancing self-confidence and self-esteem, and if the difficulty is related to work, it will need to be appropriate and feasible, and oriented towards problem solving and the positive learning that can be drawn from the situation.

To know when it is another person, rather than a different approach, that is needed

There may, however, be times when the needs of the mentee are not for a coach-mentor, but for a counsellor or other practitioner who can help them with their problems and distress. It may be tempting, when you care about your mentee and know them well, to try to fulfil this role yourself. There are two key risks here.

- Moving into a therapeutic relationship may conflict with the particular relationship or the stage in your relationship that you have developed with this individual as a coach-mentor. (There are various points of view as to whether we, in coach-mentoring, work on the same relationship continuum as a therapeutic one or whether coach-mentoring relationships are distinctly different.)
- More importantly, the coach-mentor may be working with an individual beyond their realm and level of competence, the result of which may be to cause harm to the mentee and possibly to the coach-mentor himself. If this were the case, it would be ethically unacceptable and against coach-mentoring good practice.

Note: It is advisable to discuss these issues prior to drawing up your coach-mentoring contract and to incorporate a statement that reflects what you have agreed within it.

How we help our mentee grow and develop through *change*

Another aspect that may influence the approach you use in a coach-mentoring environment relates to the change process. Many of us have read about change management, from the perspective of making change happen in organisations and about the human aspects that we need to consider.

People experiencing change may have initiated the change themselves, or the change may be externally driven. On many occasions, there is a mixture of both elements. For example, a member of staff within a department may be aware that certain enforced changes in their work area will happen at a certain point in time, but will choose to work on their personal development to take advantage of potential job opportunities that are likely to arise. Often the change processes an individual undergoes within the coach-mentoring environment are also both externally and internally driven.

The impact of change for the mentee bears some similarity to that of any other loss, and may initiate a grieving process through which the mentee progresses, enabling him to leave a familiar way of working and reconcile himself to something new.

Thus in the early stages of the learning/change process the mentee may experience a period of immobility or regression in line with the 'denial' stage of loss. As anger and frustration sets in, the mentee may berate the time that this change was embarked upon (whether chosen or not!). Finally the mentee comes to accept and, over time, gradually becomes more competent and confident in the changed way of working.

As coach-mentor we need to recognise when this process is happening, reassure and inform the mentee that these experiences and feelings are 'normal', and provide space and support within the coach-mentoring session for the mentee to address this.

References

1 Hay J (1995) *Transformational Mentoring. Creating Developmental Alliances for Changing Organisational Cultures.* Sherwood, Watford (UK), Minneapolis (USA).

2 Kolb DA (1984) *Experiential Learning.* Prentice Hall, New York.

3 Honey P and Mumford A (1983) *Using Your Learning Styles.* Peter Honey Publications, Maidenhead.

4 Mehrabian A (1970) cited in Mullins L (1999) *Management and Organisational Behaviour* (5e). Pearson, Harlow.

5 Egan G (1977) *You and Me: the skills of communicating and relating to others.* Brookes/Cole, Monterey, CA.

6 McBride P and Maitland S (2002) *Advantage. Putting Emotional Intelligence into Practice.* McGraw-Hill, Maidenhead.

7 Downey M (2001) *Effective Coaching.* Texere, London.

4

Tools and techniques for career, work and personal development

'We have more possibilities available in each moment than we realise.'
Thich Nhat Hanh

- Introduction
- Career and skills development tools and techniques
- Problem solving tools and techniques
- Personal development tools and techniques
- References

Introduction

There are a number of tools and techniques you can use in coach-mentoring, and in this chapter, I have brought together a selection for you to try and to use as a resource.

In Box 4.1, I have attempted to identify the various tools as either predominantly left-sided (logic based, LSB) or predominantly right-sided (creative, RSB) brain techniques. It is helpful to have a balanced approach to the tools you are using in coach-mentoring, so that the mentee can access a broad range of mental resources. They have also been grouped in terms of their potential use, though as with many tools, it is very likely that there are other uses they can be put to!

Box 4.1 Tools and techniques

Career and skills development
- using creative media to find out what is important to you (RSB)
- getting in touch with your value base to clarify career and work choices using the Work Values Assessment and Mapping Tool (LSB)
- your obituary – aligning your work with your life values (RSB)
- lifelines – where you have come from and where you want to go (RSB)
- future mapping – looking back from the future to identify how to move forward (RSB/LSB)
- profiling your competencies and attributes for enhancing your work and career prospects (LSB)
- using a personal SWOT to plan your future development (LSB)
- performance assessment and feedback (LSB)

Problem solving
- solution-focused problem solving (RSB)
- problem solving using the 'Five Whys?' (LSB)

Personal development
- self-esteem; working on negative beliefs; using positive affirmations; testing out a Positive Affirmation Technique (LSB/RSB)
- accessing and nurturing your creativity (RSB)
- dealing with stress at work (LSB)

Before exploring each of these in detail, please bear in mind that it is a good idea to try out the exercises for yourself before undertaking them with your mentee. Most of time, I will thus be discussing them as if you, the reader, will be working through them.

Career and skills development tools and techniques

Using creative media to find what is important to you

One way of getting in touch with how you think or feel about an aspect of yourself, is to use a right-sided brain activity. This means that you will be leaving the logical, controlling, judging part of your brain largely aside and letting the more creative, instinctive parts of your brain communicate. This may sound strange, but it is often what we do without being aware of doing it.

Have you ever listened to some music that has brought back a particular smell or taste or perhaps a picture of you at a different time in you life? Can you get in touch with some of the feelings that you had then? What kind of feelings are they? What do they make you think about that time? What significance does that have for where you 'are' now? We can use processes like this to consider what we have learned from past experiences to take us forward. We can also use them to get in touch with what we really value.

Sometimes all we need to do this is a relaxed state of mind and body. In other situations, these thoughts and feeling are hard to get in touch with and we may need some form of 'help' through using media such as music or art to help us do this. For example, you could create a 'magazine mosaic' (making a picture from paper cut or torn from magazines) of your old workplace/role/or career and your ideal one. Thoughts like 'I am not artistic' or 'this is for children' may be surfacing as you read this paragraph. But if you can suspend these and try this exercise out with a fair amount of commitment, I think what you will discover about yourself and what is important to you will surprise you.

Getting in touch with your value base to clarify career and work choices using the Work Values Assessment and Mapping Tool

Perhaps a guiding principle at work and in life in general, should be that our choices and behaviours are based on our values. However, with the frenetic pace at which we live and make decisions, this is not always the case, and the result of this can be vague discomfort or unease, dissatisfaction or outright unhappiness. Another symptom can be the feeling that 'something is missing'. At work this may be evidenced by very regular perusal of the job pages in your professional journal, or working your way through a series of different roles or jobs and never seeming to find the right one.

If you think that your values and their alignment with your work may be an issue then in addition to reflection and discussion using the more generic coach-mentoring techniques already mentioned, there as some more specific tools that you can use.

One such tool is called the Work Values Assessment and Mapping Tool. This has drawn on a range of different material on the topic of work values and on my experience of using a values wheel as a visual aid with mentees so that they can surface and compare what they are doing currently to what they value in their lives.

Applying the Work Values Assessment and Mapping Tool

Step 1 Self-assessment

Consider on a scale of 1 to 10 (1 = lowest, 10 = highest) how important the following work values are to you, then circle the score you have chosen on line (i).

Value 1. Recognition
For example, it is important to you that you:

- have a job with good opportunities for promotion
- are recognised for your work and skills by others at your workplace
- do work which is considered valuable by others?

Line (i) Score   1   2   3   4   5   6   7   8   9   10

Line (ii) Score   1   2   3   4   5   6   7   8   9   10

Value 2. Achievement
For example, it is important to you that you:

- work in a job that makes use of your strengths and work on tasks that you know you can do well
- work on a job where you can see the results of your work
- produce high-quality results, working hard to be very good at what you do
- know that the world is a better place because of the work you do?

Line (i) Score   1   2   3   4   5   6   7   8   9   10

Line (ii) Score   1   2   3   4   5   6   7   8   9   10

Value 3. Money is important to me
For example, it is important to you that you:

- have an opportunity to earn more money
- earn as much as you can
- have security of income and benefits?

Line (i) Score   1   2   3   4   5   6   7   8   9   10

Line (ii) Score   1   2   3   4   5   6   7   8   9   10

Value 4. Influence of others
For example, it is important to you that you:

- are able to supervise and influence the work of others
- have a job in which you can organise and direct the work of others
- have a job where people come to you for advice
- can influence those around you to see things your way?

Line (i) Score   1   2   3   4   5   6   7   8   9   10

Line (ii) Score   1   2   3   4   5   6   7   8   9   10

Value 5. Working with others
For example, it is important to you that you:

- work with other people towards common goals in a co-operative team
- have good working relationships with others
- work with people who have similar concerns and interests?

Line (i) Score   1   2   3   4   5   6   7   8   9   10

Line (ii) Score   1   2   3   4   5   6   7   8   9   10

Value 6. Meaning
For example, it is important to you that you:

- do work that has an impact on others
- undertake work that is socially useful and valuable
- contribute to your community?

Line (i) Score   1   2   3   4   5   6   7   8   9   10

Line (ii) Score   1   2   3   4   5   6   7   8   9   10

Value 7. Creativity/innovation
For example, it is important to you that you:

- can develop new methods of doing things, putting ideas and concepts together that have not been put together before
- can spend much of your time working out how to fix things or decide the best way to get things done
- have an opportunity to be creative and try out my own ideas?

Line (i) Score   1   2   3   4   5   6   7   8   9   10

Line (ii) Score   1   2   3   4   5   6   7   8   9   10

Value 8. Variety

For example, it is important to you that you:

- work in a number of different situations or activities needing different skills?

Line (i) Score   1   2   3   4   5   6   7   8   9   10

Line (ii) Score   1   2   3   4   5   6   7   8   9   10

Value 9. Work environment

For example, it is important to you that you:

- have pleasant, well-designed and healthy working conditions
- work in a location with good facilities, e.g. entertainment, sports
- live in a location which meets your ideal in relation to housing, transport and distance from work?

Line (i) Score   1   2   3   4   5   6   7   8   9   10

Line (ii) Score   1   2   3   4   5   6   7   8   9   10

Value 10. Work–life balance

For example, it is important to you to:

- have a job that has a regular schedule with limited or no overtime
- have a job that is flexible to support family commitments
- have a job that allows me to pursue my other non-work interests and pursuits?

Line (i) Score   1   2   3   4   5   6   7   8   9   10

Line (ii) Score   1   2   3   4   5   6   7   8   9   10

Value 11. Autonomy

For example, it is important to you that you:

- can manage yourself
- can work independently
- do things without being told what to do most of the time?

Line (i) Score   1   2   3   4   5   6   7   8   9   10

Line (ii) Score   1   2   3   4   5   6   7   8   9   10

Value 12. Stretch

For example, it is important to you to:

- be positively challenged in terms of problem solving, decision making
- test my ability to coping with adversity
- frequently work at the limit of my capabilities?

Line (i) Score   1   2   3   4   5   6   7   8   9   10

Line (ii) Score   1   2   3   4   5   6   7   8   9   10

Step 2

Mark the scores from **line (i)** for each value onto the matching value scale on the work values wheel (in Figure 4.1), and join these up around the circle so that you have a visual representation of your scores and can see your *baseline values levels* (*see* worked example Figure 4.2 overleaf).

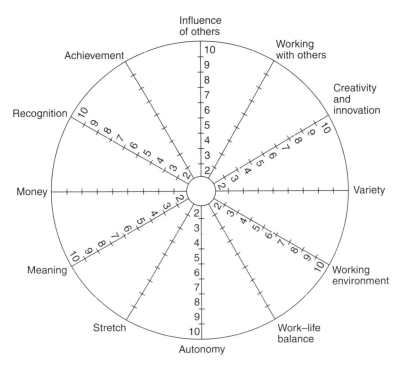

Figure 4.1 A work values wheel to copy and use for the exercise.

Step 3

Now consider your present job, how does it let you satisfy each of these values? Go back to Step 1 and circle how much each value (from 1 to 12) is satisfied in your current role/job on **line (ii)**.

Step 4

On the same values wheel that you used for Step 2 (Figure 4.1), mark the scores from **line (ii)** for each value in a different colour onto the matching values scale on the work values wheel and join these up around the circle, so you now can see your *current values satisfaction levels* (*see* a worked example of the values wheel for this step in Figure 4.3 opposite).

Step 5

Notice the similarities and differences between your own values in score (i) and how these are being satisfied at your workplace in score (ii). Then answer the questions opposite.

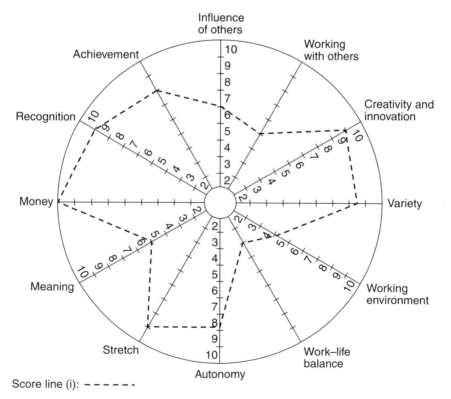

Score line (i): – – – – –

Figure 4.2   Example of the work values wheel showing *baseline values levels* from score line (i).

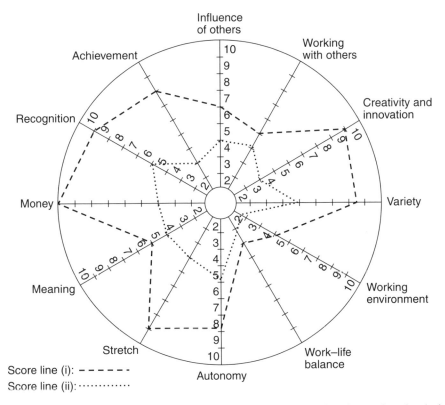

Figure 4.3   Example of the work values wheel showing *baseline values levels* from score line (i) and *current values satisfaction levels* from score line (ii).

- Which values are most important to be met?
- Are they being satisfied at present?
- If not, what would you need to do to satisfy them and which values would you accept not being satisfied in order that these are addressed?
- Are there any values and their related needs that could be satisfied other than at work, if so how?

Step 6

Identify three action points that you are now prepared to take in order to bring what you do and what you value closer together and note these down.

A1

A2

A3

Step 7

Follow these through, checking your progress on a regular basis and adjusting how these are addressed according to the changes and opportunities in your life. Always check back to your original values to make sure these are not being compromised beyond what feels right for you.

Your obituary – an exercise to help you identIfy a value-based vision for your life

Strange as it may seem, another way of reflecting on whether you are living out your values is to write your own obituary. I first came across this idea when reading Covey's *The Seven Habits of Highly Effective People.*[1] (*Note*: This exercise should not be done if you or the person you are working with is feeling emotionally vulnerable.)

First, find a quiet space where you can be alone and uninterrupted for about 15 minutes, create a mental space so that your are not worrying about your work schedule or any other demands, but just focus on the words you are reading.

Now, imagine that you are going to the funeral of a loved one. As you arrive at the building you hear the sound of the organ music, and notice the flowers and the people who are there. As you walk further in you become aware that the funeral is for you, three years from today.

You sit down and wait for the service to begin and notice on the programme that there will be four speakers there, someone from your close family, a friend who knows you well, someone from your work or profession and someone from your community. Think about what you would like each of the speakers to say about you and your life, the kind of wife or husband you have been, what kind of friend and working colleague you have been? What contributions and what achievements would you want them to remember? What difference would you have made to their lives? Note down your immediate impressions and thoughts.

Doing this will have enabled you to reach some of your deeper, more fundamental values. It should also, hopefully, have enabled you to have an image of the end of your life, which you can then use as a frame of reference or criterion by which everything else can be measured. This is what Covey[1] calls 'beginning with the end in mind'. So now that you have that clear picture of the person that you finally become, everything you do can be considered in the context of what is most important to you and selected in terms of the vision you have for the whole of your life.

Influencing your future

Now return to the notes you have made. Think about what they have revealed.

- What single thing could you do in the near future that would bring you closer to your vision?
- In the longer term, is there a more significant goal that you have identified?
- If so, what criteria would you need to put in place that would steer your future actions towards this goal?

Lifelines – where you have come from and where you want to go

Drawing a lifeline (tracing a line along a horizontal axis, with peaks for positive and troughs for negative experiences) is one way to see the journey you have taken in your life so far and where you 'are' at present. You can also think about a number of possible scenarios for the future and draw in how you think this would influence your lifeline. Take time to identify and reflect on the meaning and significance of events that have happened (to you) and look for any patterns or trends that you might have developed along the way.

The lifeline can be drawn incorporating events around work, home, social/leisure life and health together, or a separate line can be drawn for each, perhaps one above the other, so again, the interrelationship between these can be seen and considered.

Future mapping – working out what you want for the future and how to get there

The following exercise has been adapted from a process developed by Phillips[2] using visioning techniques as a planning tool. The idea is that you place yourself in your future desired state, attend to the details you can visualise to clarify that state, and then work backwards through the imagined milestones that have brought you there and what you have undertaken to achieve them. By this point you have developed a plan for moving forwards, by looking back from the future.

In more detail the process consists of three stages.

- Stage 1: Developing a clear and detailed picture of your ideal future as if you were experiencing it already.

- Stage 2: Mapping out the milestone events and achievements that took you there.
- Stage 3: Living and achieving the outcomes starting back in the present.

Stage 1: Creating the picture

- Identify the date for your desired outcome and write it down as if you are currently in that future time, e.g. today is 27 November 2007, and record any other details that you note regarding this desired state in the same way.
- What is it important that you have succeeded in? Note down what you are successful in, e.g. your skills, qualifications, position, role, organisation, income level. These are your success criteria.
- Use each of your success criteria as headings, and, behaving as if they are the list of your successes now, write down your list of achievements in the present or past tense, e.g. I am currently working as a clinical specialist in the cancer care network. I completed my MSc last year and have just been informed that I have been short-listed for a consultant post.
- For each of the achievements you have listed, write down what you see, hear or feel that would give weight to the evidence that this is real, e.g. that you can see your copy MSc certificate in your portfolio or in a frame on the wall. You can see post in your in-tray with your title of clinical nurse specialist, etc. You can hear yourself answer the phone, talking about your particular caseload and you are feeling confident about this, etc.
- Strengthening the vision helps us to clarify what we want and will motivate us much more powerfully. Ideally, Phillips[2] recommends that you need to 'mentally step into the experiences and see, hear and feel what it is to be saying and writing these things'.

The next stage is about linking the ideal future to the present.

Stage 2: Mapping out milestones and events that took you there

In this stage you need to be in the future and 'remember' what you did to achieve your success.

- For each heading where you listed your achievements, write down at least one action or outcome that had to happen to make your success in that area possible. These are the key events or turning points. If these had not happened you would not have succeeded. For example, heading: My MSc; milestone: I was accepted onto the course. Identifying these

Table 4.1 Progress chart

| | Dates | | | |
Milestones	January	February	March	April
Work-shadowed nurse consultant		×		
Obtained standard job specification for nurse consultant				
Undertook skills profiling session				
Scanned journals/Internet for post	×			
Sent for application form			×	
Submitted application			×	

turning points will help you to map out your journey to success, by identifying markers on the way. Note that these points must be written as if they are in the past and expressed in terms of what you did.

- Write down when each milestone/action took place and who was involved, if this is relevant. In remembering your success, you will find that the timing of these milestone becomes clear.
- Draw up a progress chart (*see* Table 4.1) listing the milestones on the left and the dates across the top, then map when they happened on the chart.

Stage 3: Achieving the outcomes, starting back at the present

This is about being prepared for action and following it through.

- Review your vision and keep it readily to hand in the form of charts, diagrams or written material that you can or our learner can revisit easily and regularly. Set targets and deadlines preferably through your coach-mentoring sessions so as to maintain motivation.
- Make sure that the timetable of action is in sufficient detail that you are clear about what you need to do.
- Regularly review your vision and progress and modify to keep the plan current.

Profiling your competencies and attributes for enhancing your work and career prospects

Another useful way of enhancing and developing your career, is to draw up a 'profile' of your current attributes supported by a portfolio.[3] You can then analyse your current profile in terms of how it is helping you to achieve what you want to do now and also in terms of where you want to be in the future.

The other advantage of the process we are about to explore, is that a developed and maintained 'profile' is a very clear way of showing prospective employers the specific skills, knowledge and understanding you have gained.

Sketching your current profile

Wheeler[4] suggests the following steps.

1   Decide on the attributes that are relevant to your career/job and list them within the grid below. I have filled in an example grid with a list of attributes.

Attributes relevant to my career		
Attributes	*Low score*	*High score*
Self-management		
Problem solving		
Professionalism		
Communications		
Reflection		
Teamwork		
Legal/ethical issues		
Clinical skills		
Coach-mentoring skills		

2   Now that you have listed these on a scale of novice to expert, for each attribute mark out the level of competency that you feel that you have reached.

3   With a critical friend or coach-mentor, justify with evidence the score that you have given yourself.

Level of competency I have reached in each attribute

Attributes	Low score		High score
Self-management			
Problem solving			
Professionalism			
Communications			
Reflection			
Teamwork			
Legal/ethical issues			
Clinical skills			
Coach-mentoring skills			

---

4 If necessary, make adjustments to create the agreed profile.

5 Make notes and list evidence that you could put into a portfolio for each 'attribute section'. Note that you can select the attributes for your profile from a variety of sources according to the reason why you want to profile yourself. If you are looking to enhance what you do already, then you could use your current job description or the attributes identified as clinical/ technical/managerial or other requirements of your professional association for your level and type of work. Equally, you could consider another job or career, and obtain information on the required attributes needed for this, say from the advert, person specification, job description, etc. Then create a new grid and profile yourself against this to see how closely you relate to it and where your development needs would lie. The profile allows you to see at a glance where these are. However, if this new job or career lies in unfamiliar territory, you may wish to verify the attributes and their relative importance with a person experienced in that area.

6 The final stage is to consider these learning needs (ideally with your coach-mentor) in terms of their priorities, opportunities, the time needed to address them and the likely evidence that would demonstrate that you have gained the attributes to which they relate.

Using a personal SWOT to plan your future development

The consideration of SWOT (Strengths, Weaknesses, Opportunities and Threats) was originally referred to by Ansoff,[5] as an approach for strategic organisational analysis and change, enabling people to have a framework in which to make better-informed and directed decisions in relation to their organisational objectives.

It can also be used as a tool for analysis of yourself and your environment, so that you too can make strategic decisions about your personal and career development.

Your 'strengths' and 'weaknesses' relate to you as a unique individual. 'Opportunities' and 'threats' are outside you, but part of your environment. So think about yourself and note down your strengths and weaknesses. As you do so, do not think too hard or question what you write until you have captured it on paper. This approach will allow you to capture more material and ideas, which can always be verified later if needed.

Your strengths

- What do you do well, what qualifications and experience do you have and so what skills and knowledge have you developed? What have other people fed back to you as strengths?
- What personal characteristics or attributes do you have?
- What advantages do these give you?
- What resources can you draw on?

Your weaknesses

- What do you do less well or badly? What have other people fed back to you as weaknesses?
- What strengths do you lack?
- What should your avoid doing and why?
- What disadvantages do these give you?
- What resources do you lack?

Now consider your existing environment and the wider environment in which you have the potential to interact, then think about and note down the opportunities and threats.

Opportunities

- What are the interesting trends that you are aware of – social trends, changes in government regulations, technology, events happening locally, nationally or internationally?
- Are there opportunities for training and development, market/job opportunities 'upwards' or 'sideways', in the full range of employment areas?
- Opportunities for 'time out', e.g. career breaks or travel?

Threats

- What particular obstacles are you facing?
- Are requirements/needs for your current skills changing?
- Are there risks/possibilities of redundancy?
- Are there areas of your job arising for which you do not have the skills?
- Is there threat from competition of any kind, e.g. within your workplace for promotion, entry of a new type of post or outsourcing?

Hay[6] suggests that you can assign weighting to all of these points so that it is possible cautiously 'to check the balance of assets against liabilities'. Even if you do not weight your SWOT for this particular reason, weighting it will help you to think of the relative importance of what you have identified.

Now, consider the relationship between your strengths and opportunities, weaknesses and threats. For example:

- What opportunities relate to your strengths and, for example, provide you with the potential to develop and work in new ways?
- Which of these are most feasible and how could these be acted upon?
- What weaknesses limit your effectiveness in the areas that are important to you, which of these need action to minimise or correct their effect/ how could this be done?
- What likely future opportunities/threats/changes to the environment do you need to prepare for and how will this be done?

In your action planning, consider what requires an immediate response and what needs medium-term to long-term preparation. Ensure that you plans incorporate SMART, i.e. Specific, Measurable, Achievable, Realistic and Time-based action points.

Assessment and feedback for competency development

The are a number of situations where the mentee may be working through and developing their competencies, for example while completing professional training, post-qualifying training or simply moving into a new area where several new skills and competencies are needed

Usually, if an educational facility is involved, there will be very clear descriptions of what has to be learned, applied and assessed. At other times, for example when inducting a new member of staff or learning to use new technology, this clarity may not be present automatically. However, on all occasions, it is important to develop a clear understanding of the defined level of overall performance or specific behavioural objectives, and to share these with the mentee as soon as possible. Ideally, the mentee should have an opportunity to formulate goals and expectations collaboratively.

Gathering evidence of performance competency is likely to come from a number of sources. In some forms of qualifying education, this will be clearly prescribed at the outset. In other cases, the mentee and coach-mentor may agree where, for example, shadowing and direct observation or recording on tape is acceptable, who is the most appropriate person to do this and how this can be brought to the feedback or review session. Obtaining and using evidence on performance competency enhances the richness and depth that comes from self-assessment by providing another element for the mentee to reflect and learn from. It also provides valuable material for continuing professional development portfolios.

Enhancing the feedback process

In terms of feedback, this needs to be given as close to performance as possible, to enable the learner to know the impact and effectiveness of their performance and also to assist in maintaining motivation. If there is a scheduled formal feedback session that is days or weeks ahead, it is normally ill advised to wait until this point to inform the learner of their level of competency, as this will limit the time they will have to improve. It is much better to give informal, 'formative' (developmental) feedback early in the learning process.

However, in making oneself open to feedback, the mentee places themself in a vulnerable position, open to criticism, even though this may be constructive. Thus feedback needs to be offered with considerable skill and sensitivity by the coach-mentor.

In preparing to feed back consider the following.

- Gather information for feedback carefully so as to ensure the information used is detailed and accurate.
- Make sure that when you prepare to make a point you have examples to illustrate it.
- Check that your message is clear and unambiguous.
- Deliver negative feedback in a non-threatening, constructive manner:
  - describe the action, process or issue, not the individual
  - communicate what was done correctly as well as where the problems were
  - always indicate what would need to be done to improve the performance.

- Be honest and open about current performance and where future opportunities lay.
- Mentees need time with the coach-mentor to understand the feedback thoroughly, make sure that the session is held somewhere free of interruptions and will be long enough for a detailed two-way conversation.
- Always put difficult feedback in perspective, consider options and explore possible remedies/ways forward.

Problem-solving tools and techniques

Solution-focused problem solving

This is useful to apply when you are working with someone who is so immersed in their problem that they cannot see their way out of it. Cottrell,[7] who uses this approach in solution-focused therapy, says we need to spend more time focusing on solutions than on problems, because we tend to get what we notice, so we need to notice what we want to get.

He uses 'the miracle question'.

- Imagine that tonight while you are sleeping, something like a miracle occurs. The miracle is that your problem has somehow been resolved. It is not until you wake up that you are aware that the miracle has happened.
- What is the first thing you notice that is different, that tells you the miracle has occurred? Describe in detail.
- What else is happening through the course of your miracle day?
- Who else is aware that this miracle has happened and what are they seeing that informs them that it has?

Try using these questions as a way of releasing your learner from the limited number of possibilities he has been considering as the 'only options', and see what happens.

Problem solving using Peter Senge's 'Five Whys?'[8]

This is a simple technique that can be done by yourself or with others.

When a problem is discovered:

- the first 'why' to ask is 'why did this happen?'
- for each of the answers to this question, you can ask 'why is that?'
- then to these answer(s) ask 'why?' again, until you have asked and answered 'why?' five consecutive times.

This approach, Senge suggests, is to help you get down to the root of the problem, rather than dealing with its symptoms.

Personal development tools and techniques

Self-esteem

Why is this important? Cantor and Bernay, and also Shub, all cited in Carlock,[9] state that people with high self-esteem have positive feelings about themselves that are not shaken by challenge and adversity. To have high self-esteem is to have the firm belief that people care about you, that you are special and needed.

High self-esteem comes from actualising yourself, i.e. claiming and cultivating your natural talents and resources and identifying and facing your challenges. Putting it another way, James cited in Carlock,[10] suggests that self-esteem is the degree to which one can achieve one's goals and aspirations.

To me, this seems to imply that you can have:

- positive cycles of self-esteem, whereby high self-esteem allows people to enter and meet their challenges, which further builds up their self-esteem, and this in turn encourages them to find and meet more challenges, *or*
- negative cycles of low self esteem, where poor self-esteem and self-belief encourage lack of achievement to become a self-fulfilling prophecy. Here, people do not believe they can find and meet their challenges, so they do not attempt them, thus leading to more negative beliefs about their achievements and potential.

I also believe that coach-mentoring can break into this cycle, by helping people to reframe their negative or limiting beliefs and to build up and affirm their positive self-beliefs.

Working on negative beliefs

Try the following exercise for yourself.

Think back to a time when you have stopped yourself from doing something because you did not believe you could do it. For example:

- I could not learn spreadsheets because I am hopeless at computers (a little too close to my personal experience at present!)
- I could not go for that job because I am not the right material
- I cannot tell my colleague that her behaviour is unacceptable because she will not like me anymore.

What is happening here is that negative beliefs and thought patterns are limiting our potential for positive action. It is also interesting to note that, in addition, they are putting stress on our bodies.

What we need to do is to revisit the issue and make a fresh start at framing it in a way that shifts it from a negative belief about ourselves to something that brings us into a positive cycle of self-esteem and allows us to respond in a positive way.

Returning to the first example I gave, I could reframe it as follows.

Negative/limiting belief	More useful belief	Positive action
I could not learn about spreadsheets because I am hopeless at computers	Spreadsheets are new to me, but with some patient help I could make a start	Book myself in with a computer trainer I know at the hospital and put some space in my diary to practise after the session
*Now try adding your limiting belief here and fill in the other two columns	*	*

As always, the important thing to do next is to make sure that you follow through your action points. This is where coach-mentoring is so helpful because it keeps us motivated.

Using positive affirmations

Shifting from negative language to positive language about ourselves can have an amazing impact on how we feel and ultimately on what we do and achieve both for ourselves and for other people.

Notice what feelings the following statements create in you.

- I am happy about who I am.
- I am open to receiving positive feedback.
- I am building up my personal resources every day.

Notice also that these affirmations state the desired outcome as already in the process of being achieved. In contrast to negative thoughts, positive thoughts actually increase the chances of producing positive results, and if we associate the desired outcome with a visual image, affirmations can create even greater power. So let's try this out.

Testing out a positive affirmation technique

- Think about something that you want to achieve.
- Write this down in the 'here and now' — e.g. 'I am using the spreadsheet confidently and effectively'.
- Choose something that you believe that you can do.
- Incorporate your strengths with your positive affirmations.
- State affirmations that are within your control.
- Choose action words.
- Choose a feeling word to motivate action.
- Imagine yourself in lots of different situations that relate to the affirmation as you write this down.
- Once you have written out your affirmation, repeat you affirmation several times, preferably with your eyes closed so that you can see the images that it creates.
- If you can find a picture of this image in a magazine, cut it out and place it somewhere where you will see it regularly.
- Read you affirmation several times a day and visualise yourself 'doing it'.
- Let other people know your affirmations so they are prepared for the change.

Accessing and nurturing your creativity

Several of the coach-mentoring tools we have covered incorporate creative techniques such as visualisation and using drawing and art. More generally it is useful to enhance our right-sided brain activity so that we can draw on this as a resource to generate ideas and solutions.

In coach-mentoring terms this is very useful for developing the options for GROW or different approaches to address the hurdles within 3D (*see* Chapter 2).

A right-sided brain fitness regime

Select and try practising one of the ideas in Figure 4.4 for a month and see how it affects the more creative side of your nature. If it works, see what the others do!

Dealing with stress at work

Another area likely to arise within coach-mentoring is when your mentee is feeling that life within their organisation is creating too much challenge and stress.

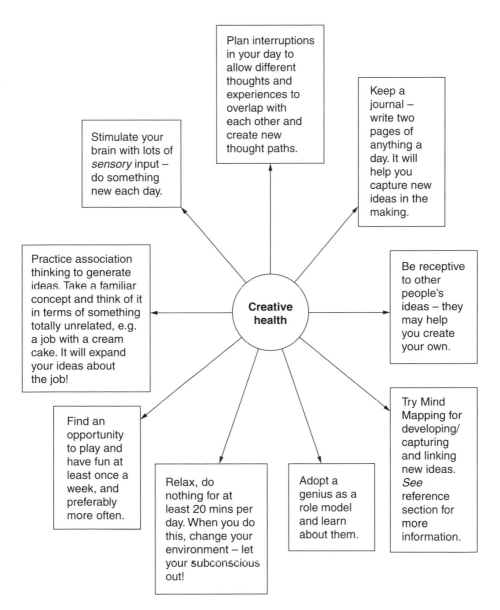

Figure 4.4   Flexing your creativity.

The following is some information and exercises on stress that you can follow within a coach-mentoring situation. As with all the exercises, make sure you are familiar and comfortable with the material before you do this.

We can define stress as the adverse reaction people have to excessive pressure or other types of demand placed upon them. Stress is now considered a health and safety risk and is a key contributor to physical and psychological ill health, increased likelihood of addictive behaviour and poor performance,

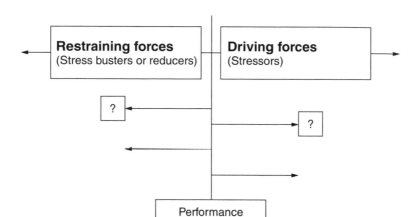

Figure 4.5 Stress force field.

which may ultimately be a hazard not only to the individual who is stressed but to other people in their care.

Whetton, Cameron and Woods[11] suggest that we can understand the dynamics of stress in terms of a force field. This is a model originally developed by Lewin in the 1950s to help consider those elements within a given situation that will act as forces to push things forward, make them happen and so cause change, and those elements that will cause resistance, pulling back and preventing things from moving forward and change from occurring.

In a stress forcefield there are 'stressors' (the causes of stress, both internal and environmental) acting as the driving forces to decrease our performance, the 'sources of resilience' that we have developed through learning and which include our coping strategies and the support that we access. Try filling in your own stress force field (*see* Figure 4.5). Add more arrows either side if you need to.

While the driving and restraining forces are in balance our performance remains unaffected. But if the driving forces become greater than the restraining forces, the forces become unbalanced and our performance changes.

Reactions to stress

As humans, our innate physiological response is to release 'fight or flight' hormones in our bodies, leading to a range of symptoms such as raised heartbeat, blood pressure and sweaty palms, as well as more positive aspects such as increased mental alertness.

These reactions are largely self-correcting if the stressor is removed. However, if the stressor continues, we move into a 'resistance' stage, where psychological defence mechanisms predominate and the body begins to store up excess energy. The most frequently used defence mechanisms are:

- aggression
- regression (return to an earlier pattern of behaviour, e.g. from childhood)
- denial (that the stressor or stress event has happened/is happening)
- avoidance (of the issue physically or mentally)
- fixation (repeating a behaviour that may have worked once but is no longer effective).

These work to reduce some of the physical symptoms, but if the pressures overwhelm these defences our available energy is exhausted and we are likely to suffer physical and psychological ill health such as depression or heart disease.

Managing stress

There are two key approaches to managing stress, which are best used in combination (*see* Figure 4.6):

- *shrinking* or eliminating your *stressors*
- *raising* your personal *resilience*.

Figure 4.6 Managing stress through shrinking your stressors and raising your resilience.

Shrinking or eliminating your stressors

The are many sources of stress, including our relationships with other people, our work situation and the competing demands for our time. Here, we will focus on how we can influence one of the most significant stressors, demands on our time.

Time demands

One of the most common causes of stress is too little time to meet the demands of the job. Experienced on a few occasions, time pressures can be motivating, but when the number of time pressures becomes considerable and they happen continuously, this is likely to have a detrimental effect on both health and performance.

It is interesting to note that too much time with too little to do is also stressful, though I am making an assumption that this is relatively rare within the health and social care sector.

Our work environment can be a considerable source of stress and trying to maintain a balance between agreed hours of work and achievable demands is a current challenge for organisations and individuals alike. In terms of health and safety, organisations have a responsibility to assess the risk of stress from this and to respond to what they find.

Example

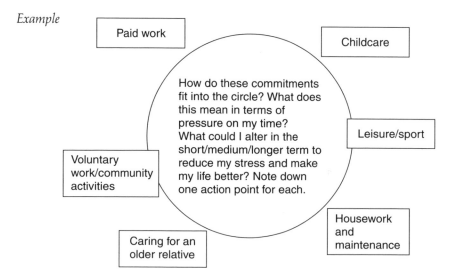

Figure 4.7 Thinking about your time commitments.

As individuals we also need to see how we can identify and manage the demands on our time through the following approaches.

- Clarifying and assessing your work patterns and workload in relation to your work agreement and job description at regular intervals, so that these can be negotiated in an informed manner with relevant line managers/human resources (HR) personnel.
- Assessing your work–life balance (WBL, the balance between your work and other activities within your life). Sometimes the time pressures on us are not only from work but also from a combination of demands to meet other commitments relating to, for example, childcare or your contribution to the community.

Box 4.2   Work–life balance tool

Use a circle diagram (*see* Figure 4.7) to break down your time into its varying commitments. Consider and perhaps discuss within the coach-mentoring session how you think and feel about the balance of your commitments, whether there is space for you to do what you *want* to do as well as what you feel obliged to. Check and challenge the must dos and ought to dos to create more options and space for manoeuvre.

- Using delegation skills when relevant.
- Developing your assertiveness skills, so as to say 'no' when necessary and not feel guilty.
- Assess and develop and most importantly keep using your time management skills.

Box 4.3 describes a simple time management self-assessment and development tool.

Box 4.3   Time management self-assessment and development tool

- Read though the techniques listed in column 1 in Table 4.2, consider/ discuss how the way in which you currently manage your time compares with these activities, marking in column 2 whether you use them or not.
- What have you noticed about the way that you have managed you time and how this has positively or negatively impacted on your performance?
- Now, think about what you would really like to improve in your time management and select up to six activities that would help you do this.

- Then identify the best way of making this happen, including allowing yourself time for making this happen and mark this in column 3 in Table 4.2.
- Plan in regular times for review in the coach-mentoring session for support and encouragement.

Table 4.2   Use of time management techniques: a self-assessment

Time management technique	Current use? Yes/No	Action required?
Do you keep a 'to do' list?		
Do you use it on a regular basis to store, sort and prioritise tasks?		
Can you name your time waster tasks?		
Do you move paperwork on each time you handle it?		
Do you keep a day, week and year plan?		
Do you make time to plan and actually use the time you set aside?		
Do you set short-, medium- and long-term goals?		
Do you use goals to sort tasks for importance and urgency?		
Do important and urgent take precedence over pressing and easy?		
Do you have strategies that protect your time from other people's demands?		
Do you plan in activities that increase your effectiveness such as:		
− networking, building relationships		
− developing new skills and ideas		
− planning		
− treats and renewal?		
Do you regularly ask yourself 'Is this what I should be doing?'		
Do you act on the answer?		

Raising your personal resilience

- In a similar way to the previous section, read though the ideas/techniques for resilience raising listed in column 1 in Table 4.3 and consider/discuss which of these you currently use at present, marking this in column 2.

- What resilience raising techniques seem to work best for you? Have you given yourself the opportunity to use them enough/at all recently?
- Are there additional ideas that you have about raising your resilience to add to column 1?
- What would you need to do to be able to use these to help yourself? Add your thoughts to column 3.
- Then identify the best way of making this happen, including allowing yourself time for making it happen, and mark this in column 3. Including dates and sharing your ideas with a friend or a coach-mentor will make them more likely to happen.

Table 4.3   Use of resilience raising techniques: a self-assessment

Resilience raising technique	Current use? Yes/No	Action required?
Identify a list of small 'treats' and treat yourself at least once a day for a minimum of 20 minutes		
Look after you body through diet and exercise		
Avoid excess caffeine, alcohol and other forms of self-medication		
Learn one or two relaxation techniques and practise them for real		
Build your social support network, developing relationships with mutual trust, honesty, kindness and respect		
Work on improving your interpersonal competencies, e.g. relating to managing conflict		
Working on your self-esteem – see self-esteem exercise earlier in this chapter		
Encourage yourself, by working on and completing one or two exercises from the 'Stress management' section in this chapter		
Use a coach-mentor to help you think through these techniques, plan for action, support and follow through		
Your ideas		

A note of caution

These are just a small selection of the tools and techniques you can use in coach-mentoring. The quality, appropriateness and understanding linked to their use is much more important than numbers or the frequency of their application. It is very tempting to use these things as an end in themselves rather than as a means to an end.

Always double-check with yourself, prior to applying a tool, the reason for its use and whether it is the best thing for your mentee's needs. If you are unsure, but think that it may be useful, then share this with your mentee and give them the option of experimenting with you in a collaborative way.

References

1 Covey SR (1989) *The Seven Habits of Highly Effective People*. Simon & Shuster, London.

2 Phillips B (1996) Future-mapping: a practical way to map out the future and achieve what you want. *Career Development International*. **1**(2): 10–18.

3 Wheeler N and Grice D (2000) *Management in Health Care*. Stanley Thomas, London.

4 Wheeler N. In: Jennison N *et al.* (2000) *Pathway to Success in the NHS. Opportunities in the Thames Valley for Mapping Your Healthcare Career*. Thames Valley Strategic Health Authority, Oxford.

5 Ansoff HI (1987). In: Mullins LJ (1999) *Management and Organisational Behaviour* (5e). Pearson, Harlow.

6 Hay J (1995) *Transformational Mentoring. Creating Developmental Alliances for Changing Organisational Cultures*. Sherwood, Watford (UK), Minneapolis (USA).

7 Cottrell S (2000) Solution-focused therapy workshop notes. From www.clinical-supervision.com (accessed 27 August 2004).

8 Senge P, Kliner A, Roberts C *et al.* (1994) *The Fifth Discipline Fieldbook. Strategies and Tools for Building a Learning Organisation*. Doubleday, New York, London, Toronto, Sydney, Auckland.

9 Cantor D and Bernay T (1992) and Shub N (1994) cited in Carlock J (1998) *Enhancing Self-Esteem*. Taylor & Francis, London and Philadelphia.

10 James W (1890) cited in Carlock J (1998) *Enhancing Self-Esteem*. Taylor & Francis, London and Philadelphia.

11 Whetton D, Cameron K and Woods M (1994) *Developing Management Skills for Europe*. Pearson, Harlow.

5

Making coach-mentoring work in organisations

'The major challenges for leaders in the 21st century will be how to release the brain-power of their organisation.'

Warren Bennis

- Introduction
- Setting up a coach-mentoring programme
- Informal versus formal coach-mentoring schemes
- Cameos of coach-mentoring in practice
- Organisational characteristics that support coach-mentoring
- Organisational benefits
- References

Introduction

Many organisational initiatives stand or fall on the time and effort given to preparation. I believe that coach mentoring is no exception. Over the past 10 years, much has been learned about this preparatory phase, and so the aim of this chapter is to share some of that learning with you and to suggest the questions you need to ask yourself *en route* to developing your own programme.

This chapter is also about celebrating some real-life coach-mentoring initiatives and considering the benefits both from these and more generally from coach-mentoring activities in organisations. These will be mentioned within the mentoring cameos and summarised at the end of this chapter.

Setting up a coach-mentoring programme

Coaching and mentoring programmes are devised and developed in many shapes and sizes, depending on the type and culture of the organisation, the people involved in leading and supporting their development, and the reason why the programmes were originally developed or have emerged.

The following are a series of detailed preparatory questions geared towards helping you develop a clearer picture of the nature of the programme you would like to have, and the key areas you need to consider in bringing this to fruition. They will focus on:

- the aim and purpose of the programme
- links between coach-mentoring programmes and existing staff training and development provision
- training, development and supervision for the programme
- life of the organisational programme, prescribed length of individual coach-mentoring sessions/frequency of meetings/relationships
- mentees
- coach-mentors
- record keeping
- pairing mentees and coach-mentors
- thinking in terms of project management
- resources
- monitoring and evaluation of the overall programme.

Questions to consider

- What need or issue are we trying to address through the programme?
- Why is a coach-mentoring programme the best way to meet our identified need?
- How can I tell whether my understanding of this matches others?
- Who can help me on this?
- Who are the key stakeholders?
- What process am I going to use to ensure that people have agreed to this and will be involved in the development process?

Aim and purpose of the programme

This may sound simple, but it may take some time to put this in a communicable form and also to be sure that your ideas and those of all other key parties who need to be involved and support this initiative, completely agree. In a large organisation, this may be a complex activity incorporating a mapping exercise of key stakeholders, drafting of proposal papers, etc.

NB Senior management sponsorship is crucial not only to initiate the project but also to help gain access to resources and surmount organisational hurdles as the development of the programme gains momentum.

Links between coach-mentoring programmes and existing staff training and development provision

Linking coaching and mentoring programmes with other training programmes is likely to consolidate learning and help people transfer knowledge into practice.

Questions to consider

- How does the programme link with our in-house training schemes?
- Is there any way of making these links more explicit?
- If appropriate, can we link our programme with staff access to external training/courses, e.g. in local higher education, to support more effective application of their learning in, say, management development?
- Are there any connections we can make with our career, succession or personal development planning systems?
- Are there possible connections with major organisational changes, e.g. restructuring, that may benefit both the individual and the organisation?
- Could it be linked with particular organisational development work, e.g. on work–life balance?
- How, in outline, would these links be created?

Training, development and supervision for the programme

What initial training and development work is needed for the:

- mentees
- coach-mentors
- line managers?

How will supervision be provided – one to one or in groups – and by whom? (*See* Chapter 6 for more information on supervision.) Who will facilitate this? What will be needed for ongoing development to motivate and enhance coach-mentoring skills – in-house/external? Who will deliver this?

Formality–informality continuum

As you consider the development of your scheme, start to think about how formal you would like its structure to be and why? Consider the questions in Table 5.1 to help you think this through.

Table 5.1 Characteristics of formal and informal programmes

Formal	*Informal*
Formal structured system	Ad hoc, self-selecting process
Detailed selection/matching procedures	Limited or no documentation
Full documentation	Few or no formal links to or control by
Formal links to HR	the organisation

Life of the organisational programme, prescribed length of individual coach-mentoring sessions/frequency of meetings/relationships

Questions to consider

- Is your overall programme to be time limited or to run on a permanent basis?
- For individual coach-mentoring relationships will the length of that relationship be prescribed (commonly up to 18 months, meeting no less infrequently than two-monthly to be most effective)?

- Will the programme be set at a maximum length in time per session (usually between 60 and 90 minutes)?
- What might influence this, e.g. time availability, level of demand on coach-mentors, views on maintenance of focus and minimising dependency, freedom for decision making at participant level?

A note of reassurance

There is no one right answer to many of these questions, what is important is to ensure that they are raised and discussed, and that ultimately the programme responds to the needs of the people it serves.

Mentees

Questions to consider

- Who is the programme targeted at?
- Is it available for all staff or a specific group of staff?
- How will you make sure that decisions about access, e.g. membership, prioritisation, etc., are fair?
- If for a specific group, will this create issues for staff not included; how would this be managed?
- What is the programme to offer them, e.g. broader personal development or specific skills, both?
- Is participation voluntary? If not, what issues does this raise and how will these be dealt with?

Coach-mentors

Questions to consider

- Who can be coach-mentors?
- Does that include line managers? If so, what are the potential conflicts of interest relating to issues such as power differential and disclosure that might arise, and how will these be managed?
- In education, does this include assessors or can this role be separated? If not, what can be done to reduce the potential dilemma of needing to reveal 'inadequacies'/competency gaps in order to learn, but fearing that disclosure may jeopardise results?

- Self-selection or selection of mentors by criteria, if so what criteria?
- How will the selection process be undertaken and by whom?
- Will there be a limit of the numbers of mentees that a coach-mentor can have at any one time? How will that relate to the hours available from these coach-mentors, e.g. a busy manager may be able to have one or two learners, whereas a coach-mentor who is reducing their mainstream work may be able to take eight to ten learners?
- Is participation voluntary? If not what issues does this raise and how will these be dealt with?
- Will all coach-mentors have to come from within the host organisation or could they come from an organisation with a reciprocal arrangement so as to broaden the range and availability of 'off-line' (non-line management) potential coach-mentors?
- Can coach-mentors be bought in from a private consultancy? If so, how will they be selected and who will manage the contractual relationships?

CIPD selection of coaches

It is interesting to note that for employing individual external coaches, the Chartered Institute of Personnel and Development (CIPD) guide for *Coaching and Buying Coaching Services* recommends a careful and detailed selection process.[1] This should include the short-listing of potential coaches, identifying two or three potential candidates who match the coachee's development needs and learning preferences. The coachee can make their choice from these candidates. Having done so, the coachee notifies HR. HR then informs the coach of their selection and draws up a contract. The coachee/HR finally contacts the coach to arrange the first session.

Record keeping

Questions to consider

- What meeting/contract records are to be held, by whom (just by the mentee or the coach-mentor or both)?
- Will a central function, e.g. a co-ordinator/administrator hold any records/details, e.g. copy contract, contact details?
- Will they be involved and hold details of any reviews or evaluations?
- How is confidentiality to be maintained/monitored?
- Is the process legislation compliant?

Pairing mentees and coach-mentors

There are many different options for matching coach-mentoring pairs, the following is to help you to explore the questions and possibilities open to you.

On what basis should pairing be done?

Despite the fact that working group members at the European Mentoring Centre Conference in 1998 came to the conclusion that there is *no* consistently reliable method of pairing,[2] they *did* agree that there was a need to ask mentees to articulate their objectives from the relationship. Also that these objectives need to be considered when seeking a mentor match.

Based on his doctoral research work, Hale[2] made the following recommendations.

- When matching, if possible seek to understand some of the fundamental values of both parties to ensure that there is no obvious clash, as this is likely to hinder the relationship.
- Mentoring relationships where the mentor is one level higher than the mentee are likely to lead to quicker development. Where the mentor is more than one level higher than the mentee, extra time should be allowed for developing rapport.
- Considering the development needs of mentees and matching them with mentors who have strengths in the relevant areas may help.
- Understanding learning styles and using a model of learning styles preferences may provide a better basis for pairing than seeking a match or contrast based on profiles.
- Regarding gender, mentees rather than mentors are likely to have different personal preferences.
- Leaving the mentee to set up the meeting may not work where there is a difference in (seniority) levels.
- Too much similarity in social type may support relationship sustainability, but may not support learning (due to the potential for collusion and comfort), and may lead to too much familiarity and lack of structure in the meeting.

Questions to consider

- What are the implications of the above points from Hale[2] on developing and implementing our programme?

- Should pairs be self-selected, appointed or should a third party such as the programme co-ordinator provide support and guidance to facilitate the pairing, but the final decision be made by the mentor and mentee?
- Should a database and computer system be used for mentees to match themselves with a possible list of coach-mentors?

Thinking in terms of project management

Questions to consider

- Who is the project manager, sponsor and project team for developing this programme?
- How/when will a project plan be developed and presented, and to whom?
- Will this incorporate a feasibility study/piloting/risk management?
- Will the plan incorporate a communications strategy, formal launch, use of media over the intranet/leaflets, etc?
- Has adequate time been allowed?

Resources

Questions to consider

- What is the potential time availability of coach-mentors, mentees and managers? How does this relate to what can be offered and when?
- Do key players view the programme as a priority for their commitment of time, energy and financial resources and how is this evidenced?
- What resources are needed to co-ordinate and administrate the programme? Will this be incorporated into existing or new posts?
- In which department/directorate will the resources be held? What implications arise from this?
- How will training relate to the project, e.g. basic training and development workshops for learners and coach-mentors?
- How will supervision be financed?
- Which potential sources of funding have been investigated?

Monitoring and evaluation of the overall programme

Questions to consider

- What will be monitored and evaluated?
- How often, when and with whom?
- What process will be used?
- Will individual evaluations feed into this? If so how?

Informal versus formal coach-mentoring schemes

Whether we consciously choose to encourage informal coach-mentoring or not, it is likely that this exists in some form or other within most organisations. Often people having created for themselves a network of developmental relationships, each of which offers different elements of support and learning in areas such as political infrastructure/astuteness, knowledge and skills development, confidence building, and so on. These are positive and increasingly essential aspects of working life that need to be encouraged. And yet how does this compare or relate to the more formal arrangements that we have been discussing not only in the previous section, but throughout this book?

Perhaps, rather than thinking we should choose either informal structures or formal structures, we should consider that they may be complementary and related to the level of development of the organisation. Let's first explore informal coach-mentoring in a little more detail.

Calling a coach-mentoring approach 'informal' may have different meanings to different people. My interpretation of this is that it could have three possible meanings.

1   The programme is not 'owned' by the host organisation and is thus not formally acknowledged or resourced as part of the systems through which it operates.
2   Some or all of the processes within the coach-mentoring activities being undertaken do not have specified processes that the participating individuals are expected to undertake on a consistent basis (e.g. no contract, no records kept, mentors and mentees self-select, no formal training, etc.).
3   A combination of 1 and 2 above.

From this, you may have observed that 'informal' comes in many shades and can lie at many points of the formal/informal continuum we drew in Figure 5.1.

Formal   Informal

Figure 5.1   Formality–informality continuum.

Informal mentoring may have advantages in that some employees may feel less reticent in coming into a less-structured and overseen process and perhaps might feel more in control. The opportunities for those participants who initiate the process are flexible and considerable, as potentially any personnel within the organisation or beyond it can be approached by another person and asked to be their coach-mentor or their mentee. The process could be speedy, as there are likely to be few or no procedures.

The key disadvantage is that the quality of such experiences is likely to be hit and miss, with a range of potential issues, from lack of clarity of objectives and relationship problems to lack of resources or line management concerns.

However, Clutterbuck[3] points out that organisations with a strong formal system also seem to develop healthy informal relationships. He states that the key seems to be that people who have experienced effective mentoring as a mentor or mentee and have been well trained, are open to a wide range of developmental alliances. Such individuals tend to appreciate the value of difference and being stretched in learning relationships and seek out challenging relationships.

The suggestion here is that once there is a seasoned body of expertise, then having informal systems where people can select and ensure the quality of their own relationships, can work comfortably in parallel to the formal one, and perhaps eventually replace it.

Clutterbuck[3] goes on to say that for such informal relationships to flourish, they will need the right environment. As he points out, the environment described has elements that you would want for a 'structured programme', which underlines the fact that formal and informal mentoring are very much part of a continuum. His recommendations are as follows.

- On-line registration and matching system, where people seek and make their own pairings with good guidance about how to select, and further advice available if possible.
- Good role models who can also provide informal advice, preferably from senior management.
- Voluntary training resources, open training programmes, in-house or external, shared by a consortium of organisations.
- E-learning package, PC or on-line, other reading resources on broad range of developmental relationships, opportunity to take formal qualifications, certificate or degree.

- Need to discourage people who have no experience/training from being mentors.
- Opportunity for mentors to meet informally for support and ongoing learning through on-line chat rooms or face to face.
- Help from HR to find venues, speakers.
- Monthly lunch and learn events.
- Good practice snippets, sent monthly to all managers/employees on developmental behaviours from mentee and developer perspective to stimulate awareness, discussion and improving skills.

Cameos of coach-mentoring in practice

The previous sections in this chapter may have helped you start to think about what you need for or how you can manage your particular scheme, but sometimes the best way to build ideas is to explore what other people have done. The next few pages include some real-life examples. See if these help and also look for other examples to expand your source of inspiration.

An Oxfordshire NHS Trust coaching scheme

The following is based on a discussion with Annie, an experienced coach and coaching co-ordinator for the scheme, in which I asked her to tell me about the key factors that made her scheme work.

Original purpose?
To introduce a coaching style to leadership.

Who accesses it?
Middle and junior managers, supervisors and team leaders – anyone who wants help to change.

What background do people come from?
Coaches come from professional groups such as finance, administration, clinical scientists and estates. The largest proportion of mentors are nurses. We have 35 mentors in total at present.

Coachees come mainly from the caring professions. Cross-functional coaching is common.

What do you think are the particular developmental opportunities of the scheme?
There is huge potential scope for people to develop using this scheme. The scheme works well for people feeling they are round pegs in square holes. Instead of losing people like this, we can help in their career development within the trust and other healthcare facilities locally.

Having the scheme available to incoming staff supports recruitment. There is an important link with *Improving Working Lives* in helping people to consider and develop their life balance.[4]

We can help people work on tackling difficulties in communication, challenging relationships and some of the complex issues common to managers within healthcare at present. Ultimately it is about helping people do what they want to do.

How is matching done?
It is done by the co-ordinator, based on an informal meeting between her and the mentee, where they explore what the coach is wanted for and the coachee's understanding of coaching.

Following this, the co-ordinator considers what she has learned from the coachee, reflects on her knowledge of the mentors and then identifies who would be make the most appropriate match. Finally, she puts people in touch and they then make their own arrangements to meet.

What training and development opportunities are available?
All coaches have a personal learning plan and meet every three months with the co-ordinator to take their learning forward. People can access a network of supervisors for support via peer supervision. They can also access the learning sets provided for people undertaking an in-house certificate in coaching.

There is a coaching partnerships meeting composed of a network of local coaches, which all coaches are encouraged to attend, and which provides valuable learning updates on coaching and opportunities to network.

Coaches are now encouraged to undertake an in-house certificate franchised by an external provider. It is a requirement that application forms are accompanied by a supporting statement from the applicant's line manager. People wishing to take this option to become coaches are first coached for three months as a 'taster', before moving on to the nine-month course.

Supervision within the courses is two-monthly on a one-to-one basis, plus participation in an action learning set.

How is the scheme promoted?
● Advertisement on the hospital email.
● Recommendations/word of mouth.
● Fliers.
● Via other development resources for staff.
● Alongside leadership training.

How is the scheme supported?
Through a small group of senior HR staff. Financial support for training has been through the Strategic Health Authority.

What resources are there for the scheme?
A co-ordinator's post, plus one-day administration support, office/computer facilities and a small library of books.

What resources are there for the participants?
People tend to do the coaching in their own time. Coachees usually have a session of one hour per month.

What systems do you have?
There is a log of coaches who email the administrator about their availability over a given number of months. The log also contains the name, phone number and site of the mentors.

Once the co-ordinator has identified a suitable coach, she will ask the administrator to check the log for the coach's availability and then give the coach's contact details to the coachee. If the coachee does not find the coach suitable, then they contact the administrator who will work with the co-ordinator to find and inform them of an alternative coach. There is also a record kept of coaches' personal development plans.

Great care is taken over confidentiality, as people have not always informed their colleagues that they are being coached.

Coaches and coachees take responsibility to maintain their coaching records.

What is the involvement of line managers?
This is not compulsory. Coachees may or may not tell their manager that they are having the sessions depending on the circumstances.

What are you most proud of?
Peoples' commitment and passion. I can see people becoming more confident and achieving more. As the co-ordinator, I have found something really meaningful, a vocation in life, something that is really me. I am proud of my administrator for setting up the systems.

What are your greatest challenges?
- Keeping it going, succession planning.
- Raising awareness at senior levels.
- Further integrating coaching into the leadership development programme.

Are there any new developments?
The latest development is a career coaching service specifically developed to help people address organisational change. The highest priority is given to offering a service to people at risk in terms of being affected by likely or imminent job change or loss.

The service is promoted via team briefings, the intranet, HR and the library. Managers can also refer their staff.

A Berkshire Council mentoring scheme

Having been involved in this scheme as an external facilitator for some of the mentor training within it, I spoke to Richard, the organisational development manager, to find out more about how the scheme is run. The following information has been drawn from this discussion, from information distributed across the organisation regarding the mentoring scheme, and also from the forms used to capture information and to help bring mentors and mentees together.

What are the aims and purpose of the scheme?
To provide an 'off-line' management-mentoring programme that provides a support framework, alongside line management, enabling and empowering managers to take control of their own situation and their own development. The scheme aims to support managers in making significant changes in knowledge, working practice and thinking required to manage local authority services effectively in the 21st century.

The specific benefits to mentees are communicated as:

- access to advice and guidance
- access to contacts and networks
- reassurance
- an opportunity to focus on areas from personal development plans and any priority areas the managers are working on
- an opportunity to create space for raising self-awareness, exploring current practice and gaining a broader personal and professional perspective
- providing a sounding board and opportunity for mutual learning.

Potential benefits to mentors are described as:

- enhancing their interpersonal skills
- gaining insight into the workings of their or similar organisations and teams
- enjoying the satisfaction of seeing others grow.

Organisational benefits are stated as:

- better recruitment, induction and retention of staff
- better communication across departmental and organisational boundaries
- faster organisational learning
- stronger organisational culture
- an effective approach for supporting and developing black and minority ethnic managers.

The scheme links with the broader strategy of self-directed learning and complements the action learning groups being developed across the organisation.

How has the scheme been promoted?
The scheme was launched in September 2003 and was fully operational in January 2004. It was promoted in a variety of ways, including via local newsletters, distribution of fliers and word of mouth.

Who participates in the scheme?
The scheme is being cascaded through the tiers of management from directors and assistant directors to front-line managers.

How is the scheme structured?
This is a voluntary scheme for all mentors and managers to participate in as mentors and/or mentees.

Matching mentees and mentors

Mentors are asked to complete a resumé and profile. The resumé details the mentor's:

- name
- contact phone number
- job title
- brief description of their roles and responsibilities

as well as providing additional information including:

- what the mentor is particularly concentrating on at work at the moment and what they intend to do in the future
- the amount of time and frequency they would be able and willing to meet with the mentee
- whether telephone or email contact is acceptable between meetings
- whether a venue at the mentor's base, the mentee's base or a neutral environment would be acceptable
- details of previous experience in mentoring or other developmental relationships
- management development activity or qualifications that could help in the role.

The mentor is then asked to look at a list of 50 qualities and abilities understood to be most valued in mentors and from these to select 15 which they feel are most applicable to them, and that they would bring to the relationship. Then the mentee is asked to identify 15 of the qualities/abilities that they feel they have most need to develop further.

Mentors are informed that the first list is used for circulating to potential mentees with the rest of the resumé information. The latter part of the list is kept confidential and is used as a basis for mentor training and development.

Mentees also are given the same list of 50 qualities/abilities and asked to identify 15 of those most important to them. They also fill in a mentor selection form with their name, job title, location and three selections for mentors in order of preference.

Two people within the human resources department have the task of matching people against the profiles, preferences and qualities lists supplied.

Frequency, number and length of sessions

- Mentoring sessions are generally held anything from monthly to every two months, for between one and two hours, in the work location of the mentor or mentee. If off-site, this is done through agreement of the mentor, mentee and mentee's line manager.
- Either party can dissolve the relationship after a minimum of three sessions. However, both mentee and mentor need to have discussed the matter together as part of their mutual learning.
- The maximum number of mentees the mentor can have is three.
- Both mentors and mentees receive training. In addition, there are regular debriefing groups with the mentors for evaluation and sharing of ideas.

What resources does the scheme utilise?
A modest amount of core funding for training and matching via HR, plus the staff time set aside for the mentoring sessions themselves.

What benefits and challenges have you identified?
The particular benefits originally identified at the outset of the scheme are already being verified by the participants. The main challenge at present is generating enough mentors.

The Acorn Scheme

This relatively simple scheme run by an Oxfordshire Primary Care Trust is an example of coach-mentoring for a specific function. Under this scheme, anyone with an idea for an organisational project can submit a proposal, which, if approved, will entitle the 'proposer' to coaching/mentoring from a senior manager from within the trust to help him achieve his project goals.

The beauty of this approach is that this is a 'win–win–win' situation, in that:

- 'proposers' benefit from being supported and steered through the complicated mazes created by organisational systems and politics
- managers benefit from being kept in touch with initiatives and having an opportunity to 'mentor' people across organisational boundaries
- the organisation benefits from the creativity this encourages and the positive outcomes gained from supporting worthwhile projects.

Coach-mentoring in education

Pre-qualifying education

Within the pre-qualifying learning environment, professional bodies and educational institutions will have detailed the requirements in relation to mentor roles and responsibilities, and the roles of other educators within the practice learning environment itself. Thus, many of the questions, which would have a range of different options for some of the other schemes described above, will already have been laid down. Different health and social care professions have differing professional requirements regarding the qualifications necessary to support students in placement learning and in their assessment. For example, in nursing, the term 'mentor' has a specific professional qualification requirement and associated responsibilities before a nurse may be recognised as being able to assess the achievement of professional competence. Mentoring within this scenario is about enabling students to learn and become competent in practice related to specific learning outcomes, and the role of the mentor will primarily focus on being responsible for the supervision, support and assessment of students. The role of the mentor also relates to enabling the student to integrate into the practice setting and being an appropriate role model who promotes evidence-based practice.

In other professions, for example in occupational therapy, physiotherapy and social work, the professional bodies are currently considering accreditation for qualified professionals who undertake assessment of practice. Role titles vary across the professions and include practice educator, clinical educator and practice teacher.

Nevertheless, you may still be asked to set up mentoring in the broader sense for one of the reasons discussed earlier in this book, such as for management development or more specifically in relation to a formal professional education and training programme. In either case, it is important to ensure that the practice learning environment is one in which:

- there are good standards of practice and collaborative working between mentors, clients and colleagues
- the environment is one in which learning and positive change is actively encouraged for all its inhabitants, particularly in relation to utilising and developing evidence-based practice
- mechanisms are in place and applied for quality assurance and audit, not only of clinical practice, but also in relation to staff and student learning
- there is a clear understanding of key local and national practice education policies and standards, resources within the practice setting identified to address these and most importantly the leadership to ensure that both policies and resources are appropriately and effectively directed.

Post-qualifying education

Some postgraduate courses have now started to incorporate the practice of coach-mentoring as a way of enhancing student learning, not only for courses focusing specifically on coaching and mentoring, but also as a way of helping people bridge the gap between learned theory and professional practice in other topics. This has a particular value in enhancing management and leadership development and in my experience is much valued by the students undertaking such courses. The following is an example of one such course.

Coach-mentoring as part of a Masters course

I have been involved in leading an MSc in Management in Health and Social Care for several years. Alongside participating in action learning sets, the students on this course are coach-mentored throughout their first year of the degree. As mentioned above, a key aim of doing this is to improve the connection between course learning and learning at work. However, it is also used to enable students to check their career trajectory and support and/or redirect this as necessary.

The mentees are provided with comprehensive material on coach-mentoring within their personal development portfolio, are encouraged to set up their contract to clarify individual expectations and commitments, and supported to access the range of self-assessment materials within their portfolio. The rest develops very much according to individual need. Feedback on this approach within the degree has generally been very positive.

With regard to setting up above the educational coach-mentoring process, the main developmental areas related to:

- identifying, developing and maintaining a group of skilled coach-mentors, where the teaching team were supported to gain coach-mentoring qualifications and to continue to access learning opportunities within this area of expertise
- development of coach-mentoring materials into a portfolio for each mentee to work through as they found appropriate
- linking learning about coach-mentoring within the individual coach-mentoring sessions with the development of students' theory and practice skills within a module covering developmental relationships and organisational learning. The aim was that students would not only have a deeper understanding of the process, but would also see how they could develop and support coach-mentoring and other developmental relationships within their own practice
- introducing and managing support and supervision for course coach-mentors
- networking with known experts in the field, to:
  - share, examine and learn from our experiences
  - consider where coaching and related activities are projecting into the future world of the work environment
  - explore and clarify where we should be in relation to this and to question what we need to do to help us to get there
- clarifying operational management and resource details, e.g. the physical facilities needed for the coach-mentoring session, time allocation within workload plan, matching students and course coach-mentors, etc.

A national public sector scheme

A very positive initiative, briefly mentioned at the beginning of this book, is the NHS Mentoring Network, which can be found on NHS The Improvement Network (www.tin.nhs.uk). This network helps put people who want to access or offer coaching or mentoring in touch with each other. It offers an opportunity for people inside the NHS and external consultants to contribute their services.

The network has a database of coaches and mentors, which supports the matching of people with relevant skills and experience. Prospective mentees fill in a questionnaire on-line, search through the database, gather initial information about their chosen mentors and make initial contact via email.

Prospective mentors fill in a 'mentor application link', send it to the database lead as instructed on the website and await a mentee contact.

The site also provides access to basic guidelines on the conduct of mentoring and details of the *Leadership and Race Equality Mentoring Guidelines*.[5]

Organisational characteristics that support coach-mentoring

Having explored some examples of how coach-mentoring schemes can run, it is time to consider an important factor that may be the difference between an emergent scheme thriving or failing, and that is the organisational environment in which the scheme is initiated.

Think about the following list and consider how closely your organisation matches the characteristics of an organisation likely to support coach-mentoring.

- People within the organisation believe that learning is an essential organisational function and fundamental to organisational success.
- Managers and leaders see developing others as part of their role and use a coach-mentoring style in their work.
- Development at an individual level and at organisational level is formally allocated resources.
- Having a coach-mentor is viewed positively by the membership of the organisation as a whole.
- Decision making has a tendency to be devolved.
- Change is seen as healthy.

It is interesting to note that although the above characteristics have been described as those that would support coach-mentoring, coach-mentoring would actually stimulate this kind of organisational environment. Thus there is possibly the potential for a spiral of positive development, whereby the more coach-mentoring that occurs, the more these characteristics develop, and the more coach-mentoring is likely to be further encouraged.

I suspect the hardest thing to do is to shift the momentum of an organisation in which these characteristics are limited. Perhaps this can be done by developing coach-mentoring initiatives in organisational pockets of least resistance until there is 'adequate mass' to influence and for coach-mentoring to become more readily accepted in other parts of the organisation. Gradually such activity could become part of the status quo.

Organisational benefits

Last but not least, it is good to remind ourselves *and others* of the organisational benefits of coach-mentoring.

- It supports challenging upwards.
- It opens up upward communication and feedback.

- It improves communications across organisations.
- It improves communications between organisations in a network.
- It helps members to develop an appreciation of the organisation's culture.
- It improves understanding of informal structures.
- It enhances awareness of roles across the organisation.
- It aids retention – through both specific support and demonstration of commitment from a senior level.
- It supports the development of key skills/competencies of the organisation.
- It encourages the development of a learning culture – habits of sharing experience, skills and knowledge, being comfortable to constructively question our actions and the actions of others.
- It consolidates and passes on organisational knowledge.
- It supports the development of a healthier, more fulfilled. more productive workforce.

References

1 Jarvis J (2004) *Coaching and Buying Coaching Services: a guide*. Chartered Institute of Personnel and Development, London.

2 Hale R (2000) To match or mis-match? The dynamics of mentoring as a route to personal and organisational learning. *Career Development International*. **5/4/5**: 223–34.

3 Clutterbuck D (2004) Making the most of informal mentoring. A positive climate is the key. *Development and Learning in Organizations*. **18**(4): 16–17.

4 Department of Health (2000) *Improving Working Lives Standard*. DoH, London.

5 NHS Modernisation Agency Leadership Centre (2004) *Leadership and Race Equality Mentoring Guidelines*. NHS Modernisation Agency, London.

6

Achieving and maintaining quality of coach-mentoring in the health and social care sector

'Quality has to be caused not controlled.'
Philip Crosby

- Introduction
- Attributes, skills and knowledge needed by coach-mentors
- Supervision and support
- Code of ethics, standards and expectations
- References

Introduction

Coaching-mentoring within the public sector is a relatively new approach, with practitioners often emerging from a variety of health or social care professions, human resources or other management backgrounds. Apart from mentorship for undergraduate healthcare students, such as of nurses, the training, development and evaluation of coaching and mentoring practice at individual practitioner level is currently neither overseen by one single pro fessional body nor regulated by government.

A genuine concern of all practitioners, clients in their care and the organisations in which coaching and mentoring practice is sponsored, must therefore be to ensure an acceptable level and consistency of quality of coaching and mentoring practice. In essence there are three, interrelated contributory factors to quality in coach-mentoring.

- The attributes, competencies and knowledge needed to be effective coach-mentors.
- The supervision and support needed to develop and enhance the coach-mentor's skills and practice and to assess/monitor its delivery.
- The code of ethics, standards and expectations set for coach-mentoring that will influence not only the two factors above, but also the broader issues of developing and delivering coaching/mentoring programmes within their specified context.

We will now consider each of these in turn.

Attributes, skills and knowledge needed by coach-mentors

The following 'building blocks' of attributes, skills and knowledge are key to good practice in coach-mentoring.

Basic or 'foundation level' attributes, orientation and skills coach-mentors

These are essential to anyone providing coach-mentoring within the health or social care environment, and create a sound foundation on which further skills can be built. Ideally, anyone wishing to be involved in coach-mentoring needs to have identified an existing orientation and some ability in these areas *before* any coach-mentoring relationship is initiated. This can be done by carefully considering each of the following areas and preferably by being coach-mentored yourself with an experienced practitioner. The latter has several advantages, in that not only can it be used to provide an external perspective on identifying your coach/mentoring orientation and abilities, but it can also be an opportunity to develop these further. Several training courses and programmes include allowing you, as a potential practitioner, to experience personal coaching/mentoring within the learning processes they offer.

There are four key groups of base-level skills that you need to practice coach-mentoring.

1 *Sound personal and interpersonal skills*

These include:

- effective listening, questioning, checking for understanding, giving feedback

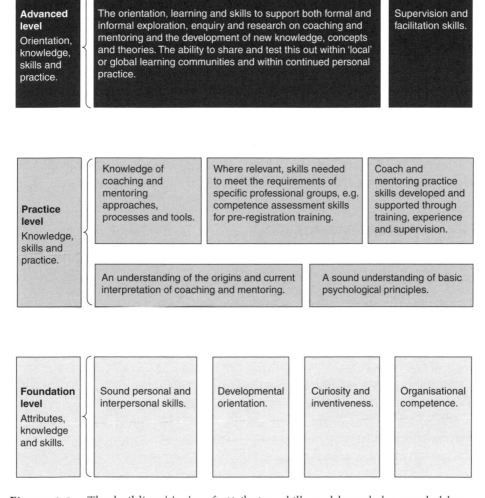

Figure 6.1   The building blocks of attributes, skills and knowledge needed by coach-mentors in health and social care.

- the ability to empathise, to tune into people's ideas, views and feelings and to encourage trust and respect
- confidence, assertiveness and the ability to challenge (or support), according to what is needed
- self-awareness in terms of understanding the dynamics within oneself as well as in others, and also so as to be able to identify and understand the implications of one's own limitations. These are essential for initiating, building and maintaining the coach/mentoring relationship (*see* Chapter 3 to explore some of these skills further).

2 *Curiosity and inventiveness*

This includes:

- an interest in and openness to new ideas and different ways of doing things, and the ability to see things from different perspectives
- an interest in finding connections and patterns, problem solving
- the ability to look forward into the future as well as back.

These are needed to help your mentee to develop their ability to reframe their understanding of a concern or its context, and to develop and expand their ideas and options (*see* Chapter 3 to consider you own creativity).

3 *Developmental orientation*

This includes:

- an ability to encourage and motivate
- an ability to relate to others based on the concept that everyone has the capacity to develop and change
- an ability to encourage personal and contextual awareness in one's self and in others
- an ability to encourage and support self-directedness and positive action
- a commitment to continue one's own development.

These are needed to help drive personal change both within the mentee and the coach-mentor, and to support personal ownership and responsibility for such changes.

4 *Organisational competence*

This includes an understanding about how groups of people, professional and organisational cultures and politics can work/influence each other. This may not be relevant to all forms of coaching and mentoring, but I would argue that within the considerably complex bureaucracies of health and social care, an ability to understand how such organisations work is an important and necessary adjunct to the other coach-mentoring competencies being discussed.

In my experience, many of the support/problem-solving needs that health and social care workers (at all levels) have, derive from an ongoing need to balance meeting the demands of multiple organisational stakeholders while trying to ensure best care to the end user and some degree of personal satisfaction. Often a coach-mentor needs to be in the position of being able to help the individual raise their awareness and understanding of what may be happening around them and to create an appropriate balance between these various demands.

'Practice' level

Knowledge and skills

These relate to the practice and delivery of coach-mentoring. You may have some of these skills already, e.g. knowledge of psychological principles, but the likelihood is that you will need to further your knowledge of coach-mentoring theory and practice in the following areas in order to offer your client a safe and effective service.

- An understanding of *the origins and current interpretations of coaching and mentoring*, to enable you to consider and clarify how you intend to apply this in your practice, and to be able to discuss this with your client. Literature on this area is growing, and can sometimes prove contradictory and confusing. Formal, particularly accredited, courses on coaching and mentoring, and organisations such as the European Mentoring and Coaching Council (EMCC) can provide guidance on the range and content of appropriate reading around the topic (*see* Chapter 1 for some basic concepts, plus the resources section within this book).
- A sound *understanding of basic psychological principles* such as those relating to personality, learning, motivation and behaviour. It should be noted that there is some debate around the degree of psychological knowledge and skills required. For example, as to whether coaches should be fully qualified chartered psychologists, have covered such learning within a coaching qualification or gained this knowledge elsewhere. Ideally, learning on this topic should be incorporated within any formal coach-mentoring training. At the very minimum, coach-mentors should assess their current knowledge and understanding in this area, identify how they will address their learning needs and follow this through.
- Knowledge regarding *the process of coach-mentoring and the approaches and tools that can be used* within this (see Chapters 2 and 3 for an introduction to these areas).
- *Practice skills* in the application of coach-mentoring knowledge through coach-mentoring training and experience, supported through supervision.

For coach-mentoring within the health and social care professions, both 'levels' of building blocks that we have discussed so far in this chapter need to go hand in hand with skills expected as formal requirements of mentoring each specific profession.

For example, in the case of nurse mentors of pre-registration students, this would involve having:

- the professional and academic qualifications that relate to the relevant part of the professional register of the NMC relating to the students group being mentored
- adequate clinical experience
- a commitment to contributing to the creation of a sound learning environment, which supports effective practice, strategies for quality assurance and the development and dissemination of evidence-based practice
- evidence of training/development to update their mentorship knowledge and skills on an annual basis, which enables them to comply with the NMC standards for mentors and mentorship. Commonly such training would incorporate the ability to facilitate learning, teaching, assessing and supporting adult learners in the workplace and will be NMC approved.

When coach-mentoring is offered, it generally incorporates the enablement of learning, potentially involving a range of learning activities and some degree of self-assessment, both as a baseline and to check progress. However, when this is offered within professional training where there is a required level of practice competence in order to ensure safe client/patient care, the content and form of this learning is more clearly specified, and the mentor has the additional responsibility of assessing competence achievement.

However, both the 'foundation level' and other 'practice level' skills we have covered above can complement these specific professional requirements and support the individual to address their learning in a way that supports self-direction and goal achievement.

'Advanced' level

Orientation, knowledge and skills

As within any other developing professional practice, experienced coach-mentors are now considering how to further advance and share their knowledge and practice. Thus, at this level, the attributes of curiosity and inventiveness are further developed into skills of research, enquiry and the development of new concepts and theories. Also there is the ability to share and test these with 'local' and global learning communities of coach-mentors and other stakeholders, such as employing organisations, clinicians, managers and educators.

Additionally, coaches working at this advanced level will need to apply new learning to their practice and develop their own skills and experience in supervision and facilitation. We explore this in a little more detail in the next section.

Supervision and support

The EMCC Code of Ethics and Guidelines on Supervision[1] require that all its members have regular supervision, although they suggest that such supervision in terms of its form, including its duration, frequency, etc., may vary according to the nature of the coach-mentoring being undertaken.

Aims of supervision

There are three key aims of supervision:

- ensuring that the supervisee's practice is professional, ethical, legal and within organisational norms
- ensuring that the supervisee is encouraged to develop their attributes, skills and knowledge in order to improve their practice
- to provide support for the supervisee when they are experiencing personal issues relating to overall work issues or their interrelationship with the learner.

Adapted from EMCC guidelines.[1]

Approaches to supervision

The kinds of approach that the supervisor may take in order to meet these aims will vary according to need and may include:

- listening and support
- assessment
- feedback
- direction
- confrontation.

Is this list starting to sound familiar? If your answer is 'yes', this is probably because we are starting to describe another developmental relationship, where the supervisee is using the supervision relationship to learn from their own experiences, both from the past and what they intend to do in the future. Done well, supervision provides an ideal opportunity for modelling the kind of relationship that we are aspiring to within our coach-mentoring practice, thus creating the congruence between practice and supervision recommended by Stevens.[2]

As in coach-mentoring, both parties within the supervisory relationship should discuss and draw up a contract which clearly defines their expectations.

Supervision contract

You should consider the following key areas for inclusion in the contract.

- Practical issues, e.g. frequency (this is often set at four- to six-weekly), duration (typically 60–90 minutes) and location. What to do/responsibilities when there are problems/changes, e.g. the need to postpone a session.
- Mentee-focused issues, e.g. around reflecting on and exploring client progress, use of strategies and techniques, intra- or interpersonal dynamics, boundary issues, ethical issues, other concerns.
- Supervisee-focused aims/objectives, e.g. developmental needs/goals, opportunity to express thoughts/feelings as a coach-mentor.
- Possible techniques to be used within the supervision process, e.g. discussion, reflection, acquiring and using feedback from clients/colleagues, use of videotaped sessions, role play, psychological self-assessments.
- Relationship between supervisor and supervisee including:
  - confidentiality
  - ethical issues
  - boundaries
  - recording/reporting
  - areas of potential concern or sensitivity.
- Time/frequency for reviewing the supervision relationship.

Forms of supervision

Individual supervision

Supervision can be done on a one-to-one basis with an experienced supervisor or can be undertaken between pairs of practitioners, sometimes known as co-supervision. In either case, it is important to find someone with whom you feel comfortable, who is also an experienced and practising coach-mentor. In accordance with EMCC Guidelines on Supervision,[1] although peer supervision (e.g. between colleagues and students) is acceptable, there should be no dual roles, i.e. the supervisor should not also be the line manager or business partner.

Working on the contract together with your potential supervisor will help provide an opportunity to consider how well you are likely to relate, as well as assessing the broader feasibility of working together. Allowing time for feedback on the supervision process at the end of sessions and a review after the first two or three supervision sessions will also help to monitor the effectiveness of the relationship.

Supervision sessions: guiding the process

The degree of structure within supervision sessions will vary and relate to the nature and preferences of the participants, how long they have been working together in a supervisory relationship and their general experience of supervision. The aim is to have just enough structure to support the breadth and depth of work needed, though to be flexible enough to focus on the supervisee's particular needs at any one time.

The style of supervision, and the degree of challenge, support and direction will also depend on the needs of the supervisee at any one time.

As we are seeking to use a coach-mentoring approach, the supervisee will set the agenda. This is likely to have a considerable focus on their mentees, but as a developmental process, supervisee learning and subsequent behavioural changes should also be encouraged throughout the sessions.

Supervision session prompts

The following key, and often interrelated, elements are likely to influence the coach-mentoring relationship and the subsequent learning and development of client, supervisee and supervisor. Developed from Hawkins and Shohet's ideas,[3] they are thus meant to provide a series of prompts rather than a rigid structure for the sessions.

1 The context (e.g. organisational, social, cultural) of the relationship with the mentee, how the relationship was initiated, the environment in which it has developed, the relationship between the client's context and that of the coach-mentor.
2 The contract (goals, ground rules, etc.) within the coach-mentoring relationship. (Prompts 1 and 2 are useful when talking about a mentee for the first time to raise contextual awareness, but will probably not be necessary in subsequent discussions.)
3 The specific problem(s) the mentee has asked for help with, the way they present the issues and the choices that they are making.
4 Thoughts/feelings the coach mentor (supervisee) is experiencing about the mentee and what that may be informing the coach-mentor about the mentee's issue(s).
5 The relationship between mentee and coach-mentor (supervisee), conscious dimensions explored, surfacing dynamics that might be occurring at a less conscious level. Consideration of what the coach-mentor (supervisee) may have absorbed from the relationship with the mentee and how this may be playing out within the supervision relationship.

6   Key strategies and interventions being used by the coach-mentor (super-visee), how and why they have used them and what else they may have done.

7   Consideration/assessment about the progress/challenges and why this is thought to be the case.

8   Reflection/discussion on what action the coach-mentor (supervisee) should take next within the coach-mentoring relationship and for themself.

9   Feedback about how the supervision session went and how either participant could improve this.

Group supervision

This is another, potentially very effective, approach to supervision that can provide many rich and different perspectives on coach-mentoring practice. Working in groups is not for everyone, and needs careful management and facilitation in order to maximise benefits and minimise any negative impact from personal exposure, group dynamics and time limitations.

As in individual coach-mentoring, it is important for the group agenda to be agreed, clarifying how participant supervisees will have the opportunity for their needs to be met within and over a given number of sessions. This in itself will impact on the size of the group, and the duration and number of sessions to be agreed. A reasonable standard would be to have a group of six to eight people meeting for approximately three or four hours every four to six weeks.

Action learning-style group

For new groups, where structure can help to reduce anxiety and help make good use of time, the following action learning-style format may be helpful to follow.

It is useful to allow space at the beginning of the session for members to reconnect with the rest of the group and to share their current interests and concerns. Following this, depending on the time available, two or more members will present their issues to the group in the following manner.
Note: Allow 45 minutes to one hour for each presentation.

- The supervisee presents a summary of their case and the specific issues on which they need help from the group (consider Supervision session prompts points 1–7 above to stimulate thinking on where the core issue lies – remember that time will be limited, so be selective).
- Group members ask for more information and ask questions to help the supervisee gain more clarity.

- Group members then give their thoughts, understanding and ideas on the issue, which the supervisee notes down.
- During a break period of about 10 to 15 minutes, the supervisee reflects on what the group members have said and prepares to feed back to the other group members.
- Following the break the supervisee responds to each group member's ideas and suggestions, in terms of how these might relate to/inform their actions regarding the coach-mentoring issue.
- The group discusses the process that they have just gone through and their learning from this.

Group facilitation

This kind of supervision works best with a facilitator, whose role is to:

- help the group keep to time and agenda
- support a balanced number and length of questions and answers
- positively direct the dynamics of the group
- stimulate individual participants and the group as a whole in their learning and development.

The facilitator can either be drawn from the supervision group membership on a rotational basis or can be 'brought in' as someone external to the supervision group, their work areas or the whole organisation. When considering an internal or external facilitator, the pros and cons need to be thought through. An internal facilitator, is likely to be familiar with the working context, will gain the opportunity to develop their experience of group supervision and there are less likely to be additional costs associated with 'buying in' an external person.

However, an internal facilitator may have relationships with group members outside the supervision group, which could affect the dynamics within it and will miss an opportunity for their own supervision while they have to facilitate. In addition, not having an external person within the group may reduce the potential for being discriminating about the supervisory/facilitation skills of the facilitator. It could also increase the potential of 'group think', which in turn may encourage greater risk-taking behaviour.

Peer group assessment

Another variation of group supervision is where all group members focus on a particular area of practice, e.g contract development or action planning. The group agrees standards and criteria for this area and then each individual member of the group details their practice, e.g. through reviewing specific cases. The group appraises these and gives feedback and guidance to the individuals concerned. The facilitator can also be involved as an expert resource.

Again, the vulnerability of group members in being open to criticism, even though this is intended to be constructive, needs careful preparation and delivery by all participants, especially the group facilitator.

Preparing yourself for supervision

Whatever form of supervision is available, there are a number of things that a supervisee can do to get the most out of them. The following are a list of suggestions and comments adapted from Mead, Campbell and Milan[4] and Barrett.[5]

- That you choose things to take to supervision that are personal and important to you, not what you think will be perceived as interesting.
- Though there may be no fixed agenda, take time, in advance, to reflect on your practice and identify what is puzzling, pleasing, annoying, confusing and surprising you in advance.
- Keep a diary of your reflections arising from the above and from your supervision meetings. You can also record the results of any actions agreed from previous supervision sessions. Keeping a diary will help you to review your learning and development over the longer term.
- Use your notes from client sessions to help you recall what you want to talk about in supervision.
- Think about the kind of help you need from supervision – you are the expert in knowing the kind of help you need.
- Trust in the experience, skills and intuition that you bring to supervision and be open with others. You have many resources to bring to group and individual supervision.

To me, the last comment emphasises the need to balance the knowledge of the gaps in our skills and experience with the celebration of all that we have learned and can share with others. It is with this mindset that we can gain most from supervision.

Code of ethics, standards and expectations

As any brief search of the Internet will reveal, there are numerous organisations providing coaching and mentoring services. There are also a number of organisations that have emerged in order to develop and promote coaching and mentoring as a profession in its own right, and to attempt to regulate the activities of their members. *See* Appendix 2 for listed examples.

One such organisation, the European Mentoring and Coaching Council (EMCC), which is well known within coaching and mentoring circles, has developed an ethical code and standards for mentoring programmes, and is currently refining a specific set of standards relating to the key competencies that are required for coaching and mentoring professionals (due for completion in 2005). It is likely that these will indicate the core competencies needed for all practitioners and the competencies required for specialist areas such as in performance and life coaching. The EMCC ethical code covers the following areas.

- **Competence**: expecting practitioners to acquire and maintain an appropriate level of knowledge and competence and to engage in supervision in order to do this.
- **Context**: this relates to understanding and relating the coach-mentoring to the context in which it takes place in appropriate manner, including developing a shared understanding of how the needs of the organisational sponsor and client will be met.
- **Boundary management**: this relates to ensuring the practice is only undertaken within the coach-mentor's area of competence, and that where it is identified that the client's needs go beyond the competence of the coach-mentor or that different competencies are needed, then the coach/mentor will refer on. Also to identify and manage any potential conflicts of interest quickly and without detriment to the client.
- **Integrity**: this incorporates the requirement of client confidentiality, disclosing only in accordance with what has been agreed with the client unless the coach-mentor believes that there is serious danger to the client or others if the information is withheld. Also for the coach-mentor to act within the law, and not associate in any way with others conducting dishonest, unlawful, unprofessional or discriminatory behaviour.
- **Professionalism**: this directs the coach-mentor to:
  - follow the client's agenda of learning and development
  - not exploit the client in any way, including in financial, sexual or other matters, and not to extend the relationship beyond what is needed
  - be aware that beyond the end of the coach-mentoring relationship there will still be a need to keep information confidential and records secure, not exploit the former relationship and provide any follow-up as agreed
  - demonstrate respect for other approaches to coaching and mentoring
  - not claim others' work or views as their own
  - ensure that their competence and qualifications are clear and not make any misleading claims in any published material.

Standards for mentoring programmes

The EMCC has set standards for mentoring programmes around:

- clarity of purpose
- stakeholder training and briefing
- process for selection and matching
- processes for measurement and review
- maintaining high standards of ethics
- administration and support.

Much of the good practice advised here has been discussed elsewhere in this book, in particular in Chapters 2 and 4.

For further details of the EMCC conduct code and standards see www. emccouncil.org.

References

1 European Mentoring and Coaching Council (2004) Guidelines on Supervision: an interim statement. From www.emccouncil.org

2 Stevens P (2004) Coaching supervision. www.trainingjournal.com *Focus*. **January**: 18–19.

3 Hawkins P and Shohet R (1989) *Supervision in the Helping Professions*. Open University Press, Buckingham.

4 Mead G, Campbell J and Milan M (1999) Mentor and Athene: supervising professional coaches and mentors. *Career Development International*. **4**(5): 283–90.

5 Barrett R (2002) Mentor supervision and development-exploration of lived experience. *Career Development International*. **7**(5): 279–83.

7

Where now?

'The art of life lies in a constant readjustment to our surroundings.'
Kakura Kakuzo

- Introduction
- Coaching and mentoring: becoming part of the infrastructure of health and social care
- Continuing to assess the benefits of coach-mentoring
- What now for you, the reader?
- References

Introduction

So far we have explored:

- the roots of coach-mentoring and how ideas about it have developed over time
- a structure for coach-mentoring and how you can apply coach-mentoring principles and techniques
- the questions you need to consider when setting up coach-mentoring within an organisational environment, and some people's experience of doing so
- the importance of quality in coach-mentoring and how you can maintain and improve it.

In this final chapter, I would like to help us look to the future in terms of how coach-mentoring is becoming integrated within our health and social care environment, and consider what needs to happen to support its further development.

I would like to end by giving you the opportunity to consider the most important question: 'What, in all that you have read, has meaning for you?'

Coaching and mentoring: becoming part of the infrastructure of health and social care

There is no doubt that the terms 'coaching', 'mentoring' and indeed 'coach-mentoring' are becoming common parlance within health and social care. Coaching and mentoring is being put to a multitude of uses, such as supporting the career development of minority groups and encouraging the development of teams that have perhaps become 'stuck' in terms of their working relationships or their interventions with service users. Mentoring, long incorporated within nurse education, is now highly favoured to support the development of senior executives and practitioners, and is starting to permeate through a much wider tranche of health and social care workers.

In organisational terms, there is potential for the threads of individual learning to be connected and interwoven so that the whole organisation can benefit. Such a state is sometimes referred to as a 'learning organisation'. Within this scenario, all learning, whether deliberately initiated or incidental, becomes linked to the organisational systems that help the organisation achieve its goals and do the things that it was set up to do. A special property of organisations functioning like this, is that not only do they help people and the organisation learn to work effectively in stable environments, but they also enable them to be responsive and change when the world around them is in a state of flux.

However, enabling learning takes conscious effort from organisations and is not without difficulty and hazards. There is significant risk that, for example, mentoring schemes may exist on paper but not in practice, perhaps because schemes are not well devised, set up or given the resources essential to allow them to work well or to survive. Remember also the commitment needed for quality and continuous development to ensure that the range of learning opportunities and developmental relationships are supported by the people best equipped to do the job.

To embrace coach-mentoring (and other developmental) relationships and connect these with organisational learning also requires a significant cultural shift. This is clearly demonstrated by the health and social care sector's current struggle to communicate convincingly the exposure of people's vulnerability to make mistakes as a truly acceptable and *safe* starting point for learning and positive change. At the same time, they are required to walk the narrow divide between 'name and blame' and ensure accountability.

Another factor, if we bear in mind the concept of each individual creating a whole range or 'constellation' of developmental relationships or 'developmental network',[1] is that we need the kind of organisations/host sectors that will support such networking. This is clearly a challenge in the often still hierarchical organisations within the social and healthcare public sector. Smaller organisations that are now emerging as part of these, or are aligned to them, will perhaps find it easier to develop networks for learning alongside or within the networks they require to function in more general terms.

For larger, more traditionally structured organisations, a particular mind-set or orientation will be needed to deliberately facilitate these networks. Creating learning/career development links that cut across various levels and organisational functions, e.g. between practitioners and managers and between organisations whether statutory or non-statutory, are examples of such facilitation. Additionally, we need to create links across professional groups as well as within them, and to identify and support leaders to champion these initiatives and follow them through.

Professional organisations are also starting to take the initiative to promote and support coaching and mentoring, and can be a useful resource from which developmental networks can be expanded. Professional networks have the advantage that members are likely to come from a range of different working environments, roles and levels. These days, different professional organisations are also creating networks between each other, thus facilitating another opportunity for cross-disciplinary opportunities.

Professional organisations are particularly valuable, as people are likely to have a number of career cycles within their working lives and thus cannot be entirely dependent on one employing organisation to provide all the developmental relationships that they will need.

Continuing to assess the benefits of coach-mentoring

There is still the need for further research into the benefits of coaching and mentoring within the health and social care sector, though current literature indicates that these seem to be about enhancing learning and professional development, and helping to address problems around motivation, communication, job satisfaction, retention of staff and overall performance.[2] The beauty of coaching and mentoring is its flexibility, and thus its ability to be put to many uses,[2] although its benefits will remain poorly supported unless there is specific action to evaluate them, most importantly by the people and organisations who initiate/host such activity and also by those committed to furthering our understanding of these developmental relationships.

What now for you, the reader?

Perhaps the main question is about deciding, in light of the discussion above and in previous chapters, what your *own* views and judgements about coach-mentoring are, their implications and what you are going to do about them.

Perhaps a guided reflection at this point might be useful. Take a moment to revisit what you have read. Perhaps flick back through the book and ask yourself the following questions.

- Is there potential to use any of the concepts that I have discovered within it?
- What did I find particularly significant?
- How does this relate to what is important to me at present?

For example:

- Has this made you think of being coach-mentored/becoming a coach-mentor or using coach-mentoring principles in the way that you supervise or lead?
- Do you want to enhance or increase your development/developmental network to further your learning or develop your career?
- What does this mean in terms of your future actions; are there some options you could explore?
- If you have selected an option(s), how could you turn this/these into **S**pecific **M**easurable **A**chievable and **T**imed action?

Having chosen your course of action, share it with someone in your developmental network and see how you can turn this into reality.

And finally ... given the time, the skills and opportunity to do it well, developing yourself and others through coach-mentoring can be an amazing and life-changing experience that will stay with you forever. I hope you have an opportunity to do this and a chance, as I have, to enjoy it to the full.

References

1 Cooper CL and Burke RJ (eds) (2002) *The New World of Work. Challenges and Opportunities.* Blackwell, Oxford.

2 Dancer JM (2003) Mentoring in healthcare: theory in search of practice? *Clinician in Management.* **12**: 21–31.

Appendix 1

Coaching and mentoring definitions

Mentoring

'Off-line help by one person to another in making significant transition in knowledge, work or thinking.' From the European Mentoring Centre, referred to in Clutterbuck.[1]

'Mentoring is a partnership between two people built on. It is a process in which the mentoring offers ongoing support and development opportunities to the mentee. Addressing issues and blockages identified by the mentee, the mentor offers guidance, counselling and support in the form of pragmatic and objective assistance. Both share a common purpose of developing a strong two-way learning relationship.' Sweeney, in Clutterbuck.

'A process which supports learning and development, and thus performance improvements, either for an individual, team or business.' Parslow and Wray[2]

Coaching

'Coaching is unlocking a person's potential to maximise their own perform-ance, it is helping them to learn rather than teaching them.' Whitmore[3]

'The art of facilitating the performance, learning and development of another.' Downey[4]

'A collaborative, solution-focused, results-orientated and systematic pro-cess in which the coach facilitates the enhancement of work performance, life experience, self-directed learning and personal growth of the coachee.' Grant[5]

References

1 Clutterbuck D (2001) *Everyone Needs a Mentor*. CIPD, London.

2 Parslow E and Wray M (2000) *Coaching and Mentoring: practical methods to improve learning*. Kogan Page, London.

3 Whitmore J (1992) *Coaching for Performance. Growing People Performance and Purpose.* Nicholas Brealey, London.

4 Downey M (1999) *Effective Coaching.* Texere, London.

5 Grant A (2000) In: Jarvis J (2004) *Coaching and Buying Coaching Services: a guide.* CIPD, London.

Appendix 2

Useful resources

Professional bodies

Association for Coaching: www.associationforcoaching.com
Association for Professional Executive Coaching and Supervision: www.coachingsupervision.co.uk
Coaching Psychology Forum: www.coachingpsychologyforum.org.uk
European Mentoring and Coaching Council: www.emccouncil.org
International Coach Federation: www.coachfederation.org.uk

Examples of providers of training and education on coaching and mentoring

Centre for Coaching: www.centreforcoaching.com
Chartered Institute of Personnel and Development: www.cipd.co.uk/train
City University: www.city.ac.uk/conted
Clutterbuck Associates: www.clutterbuckassociates.co.uk
National Health Service University (NHSU): www.mhsc.org.uk
Oxford Brookes University: www.brookes.ac.uk/schools/education/
    macoachment.html
Oxford School of Coaching and Mentoring: www.oscm.co.uk
Peter Bluckert Coaching: www.pbcoaching.com
Sheffield Hallam University: www.shu.ac.uk

Other useful organisations

British Psychological Society: www.bps.org.uk
Coaching and Mentoring Network: www.coachingnetwork.org.uk
ENTO, The Learning Network for Assessors and Verifiers: currently developing national occupational standards for those delivering and providing coaching and mentoring in a learning environment. For more information contact maggieberrie@ento.co.uk; tel: 0141 887 4706.
European Mentoring Centre, Burnham House, Burnham, Buckinghamshire SL1 7JZ, tel: 01628 661667; www.mentoringcentre.org

The Mentor Directory: www.peer.ca/mentor, includes links to other mentor sites.

Mentors Forum: www.mentorsforum.co.uk, for contacting and talking to other mentors.

National Mentoring Network UK: www.mnm.org.uk

NHS Improvement Network: www.tin.nhs.uk, provides information on mentoring and offers people the opportunity to mentor or be mentored via their database matching service.

Further reading

Alder H (1994) The technology of creativity. *Management Decision.* **32**(4): 23–9.

Beech N and Brockbank A (1999) Power/knowledge and psychosocial dynamics in mentoring. *Management Learning.* **30**(1): 7–25.

Buckingham M and Clifton DO (2001) *Now Discover Your Strengths.* Free Press, London.

Burton J and Launer J (2003) *Supervision and Support in Primary Care.* Radcliffe Medical Press, Oxford.

Caplan J (2003) *Coaching for the Future.* Chartered Institute of Personnel and Development, London.

Claxton G and Lucas B (2004) *Be Creative. Essential Steps to Revitalize Your Work and Life.* BBC Worldwide, London.

Clutterbuck D and Ragins BR (2002) *Mentoring and Diversity. An International Perspective.* Butterworth Heinemann, Oxford.

Cunningham I and Dawes G (1998) *Exercises for Developing Coaching Capability.* Available from Plymbridge Distributers Ltd, Estover, Plymouth PL6 7PZ. Contains 'a comprehensive introduction to the strategies and processes of coaching with substantial material for overheads and course notes, detailed guidance and 32 exercises to learn the role of learner, coach and observer, facilitation material.'

Garcarz W, Chambers R and Ellis S (2003) *Make Your Healthcare Organisation a Learning Organisation.* Radcliffe Medical Press, Oxford.

Landsberg M (1996) *The Tao of Coaching.* HarperCollins, London.

McFadzean E (1999) Encouraging creative thinking. *Leadership and Organisational Development.* **20**(7): 374–83.

Roberts A (2000) Mentoring revisited: a phenomenological reading of the literature. *Mentoring and Tutoring.* **8**(2): 145–68.

Rogers J (2004) *Coaching Skills: a handbook.* Open University Press, Maidenhead.

Rosinski P (2003) *Coaching Across Cultures. New Tools for Leveraging National, Corporate and Professional Differences.* Nicholas Brealey, London.

Whitworth L (1998) *Co-active Coaching: new skills for coaching people towards success.* Davies-Black, California.

Work Foundation (formerly the Industrial Society) provides various reports relating to coaching and mentoring, e.g. No 63 Coaching and No 111 Coaching and Mentoring. Contact tel: 0870 165 6700.

Zander RS and Zander B (2000) *The Art of Possibility. Transforming Professional and Personal Life.* Harvard Business School Press, Boston, MA.

Index

Page numbers in *italics* refer to figures.